The Veil Between
Two Worlds

The Veil Between Two Worlds

A Memoir of Silence, Loss,
and Finding Home

Christina Vo

SHE WRITES PRESS

Published 2023
Printed in the United States of America

Print ISBN: 978-1-64742-397-1
E-ISBN: 978-1-64742-398-8
Library of Congress Control Number: 2022915349

For information, address:
She Writes Press
1569 Solano Ave #546
Berkeley, CA 94707

Interior design by Katherine Lloyd, The DESK

She Writes Press is a division of SparkPoint Studio, LLC.

To my mother, my father, and my sister,
and my soul friend.

For our journey together in the physical
and spiritual realms.

Introduction

I never expected to find a home in Santa Fe.

For so long, I'd lived the storyline of loss and separation. For so long, I'd struggled with the concept of home. My mother's death when I was a teenager had fractured my understanding of my relationship to my immediate family, to myself, and to others. My father was emotionally distant. We didn't have much of a relationship; in fact, we barely spoke. I wasn't close to my sister, either. My family dynamics created a certain air of independence for me, but the truth was that I had become overly reliant on myself, fabricating a narrative in my mind that nobody else could be there for me.

In my twenties, I lived in Vietnam, Switzerland, and the UK, often moving every one and half years. While I lived most of my thirties in San Francisco, I wasn't sure I was satisfied there. The year I turned forty, I'd lived twenty-five years without a mother; both milestones were significant. Three months before my fortieth birthday, my sister had a health scare and was placed in a medically induced coma. During that year, so many questions about my life arose to the surface: How did I feel about being single and childless at forty? How did I really feel about my life in San Francisco? And who I had become?

The Veil Between Two Worlds

I remembered a friend's mother—a woman who was a mother figure to me—who wanted me to find a man and settle down but once told me that I was scared to do it. She believed it was because I was left behind by my mother, and I didn't want the same thing to happen if I had children. Maybe she was right, but there was also a part of me that loved my freedom, and honestly, I could only remember one moment—a point in my late twenties—when I'd thought I wanted to have children.

What was on the other side of the wounds was healing, but also more—a deeper understanding of others and an ability to see the wounds of their souls as well. As I began to connect with my own soul, I could see more clearly the journey of others' souls, particularly those who were close to me. I could see in them what I saw in myself: a desire to connect with one's authentic self.

In Santa Fe, and New Mexico in general, I started to recognize the deep connection that I had to the land, to Mother Earth, and to the maternal energy within me. Grounding was so necessary for my own personal healing. I began to feel that energy was the turning of the tides, the balancing of our planet, a shift toward feminine energy being recognized for its true power to unite, heal, and transform everything around us into love, compassion, and generosity. And I celebrated—because I'm convinced that only when the world fully recognizes all that the feminine, in its truth and complexity, has to offer can we find a more natural, peaceful balance.

Throughout my first year in Santa Fe, out-of-town friends came to visit. I watched as they fell in love with New Mexico themselves. Even if they didn't call it healing, it was clear that was what was happening for them in Santa Fe. One friend had just lost her father. One was going through a divorce. Another simply needed a break from all the responsibilities of being a mother and running a practice during COVID. Another dear friend, Kate, whom I hadn't seen for a decade, was overwhelmed by the demands of her company, a successful marketing business. She came to visit twice in one year.

One evening while having dinner with Kate and her boyfriend, Carl, during their second visit, I told them that I had a new spiritual gift that I hadn't shared with anyone. I said I could see people's wounds and the ways in which they needed to heal.

Carl put me on the spot. "Okay," he said, "tell me about myself. What do you need to know?"

I asked him to tell me about his family history, so he did—he spoke of his parents' divorce, and he spoke of his grandparents—and in the vibration of the words, I felt his wounds. It was a short moment. I didn't even say much to him but I knew those wounds needed to be healed, and once he had spoken them aloud—once he'd given them even that small amount of nurturing attention—his tone softened. His energy shifted. His normally loud and outspoken personality became tempered with a more gentle energy.

He told me that I needed to do something with my newfound gift, but I didn't want to make this into some sort of spiritual business. I just wanted to understand it and, after having relied on so many teachers and guides and therapists and coaches to navigate my spiritual journey and unravel my psychological wounds and personal blocks, to claim greater authority in my own spiritual life.

After an Akashic Record reading I had (one of a few readings I had over the course of my healing journey), the reader told me that I was drawn to the land because in a past life, in a time when my spirit had been all-seeing, I'd lived in New Mexico. At this point of my journey, she said, I was seeking creative expansion and expression. I decided at that moment, and again after the conversation with Carl, to learn to read the Akashic Records on my own—to learn to connect more deeply to my own guides rather than rely upon others in order to receive that information.

The Veil Between Two Worlds

By going through my wounds, I found spiritual authority and a home within myself. While I will always recognize and appreciate all those I've turned to for guidance and help in healing in my life, I find great satisfaction in knowing that I have become my own guide home.

Part One:

HOME

Chapter 1

Restless Soul

Since arriving back to my San Francisco apartment, I'd woken up every morning on the ground. In the middle of the night, wrestling with discomfort and unable to sleep, I'd throw my white down comforter onto the floor and wrap myself in it. The hard wooden floor was comforting and secure.

Convinced I was leaving San Francisco for good in 2019, I'd given away my mattress, and now I was using an IKEA pullout sofa as my bed. I hated it. On the few nights my housemates were out of town, I asked if I could try out their beds to see if I could sleep through the night, but still I ended up on the floor. I was drawn to the ground, though I didn't know why.

The few friends I mentioned this to seemed unfazed by my confession. Many people prefer to sleep on the floor, more than one said. Then they'd drop the name of some other friend or acquaintance they knew who slept on the floor or on a mat. "It's better for your back," one friend added. But I didn't have any back issues.

My friend Terra, who's a spiritual teacher and coach, did say something that stood out to me: "Maybe your body is calling to be closer to land."

It wouldn't be until months later, when I found myself in the New Mexico desert, as close to land and as comforted by it as I had ever been, that I would realize how much truth there was in her observation. Something deeper was calling to me—but at the time, I didn't know what it was or how to decipher the message.

I'd turned forty fifteen months earlier, in October 2019. Itching for change and potentially to find a new home, I'd gone to Ojai, where I'd stayed for three months, and then to Santa Barbara, which had turned into a six-month stay. By the time I'd returned to San Francisco in the summer of 2020, the pandemic had been in full swing. I'd been gone a full nine months, and the place felt both comforting and foreign. Back in my rent-controlled Noe Valley apartment, the only thing I had to do was figure out what was next for me.

I'd always been a restless soul—searching and longing for something more than what was right in front of me. After losing my mother to cancer when I was fourteen years old, I'd told myself to live lightly—to never be too attached to people, places, or things. The pain and grief associated with her loss were unfathomable for my teenage mind, too much to handle. Maybe an idea was planted deep in my subconscious that it was easier to be the one who leaves, rather than the one who is left behind. As I got older, I was self-aware enough to understand that this desire to flee was more about what was going on in my inner world than the external environment, but the desire itself remained strong.

Now, after having lived in San Francisco for almost a decade, the restlessness reared its ugly head once again. I needed to resolve whatever it was that was coming up for me, pushing me to leave.

I was unsure, though, if this was my pattern or if it really was time to go. I lived a relatively free life compared to others my age.

I wasn't locked into a family, a job, a business, or a relationship. I could move anywhere I wanted. Yet I felt stuck, trapped by the life I had created in San Francisco.

The whispers of my nomadic soul became a constant, too much to ignore. This was different from the wanderlust I'd experienced in my early twenties. Maybe it was an early midlife crisis. Whatever it was, there was a deeper yearning for change than there had been the first time I left.

Finding myself back in San Francisco that summer, I faced a conundrum: I'd told my closest friends I wouldn't be returning, and yet here I was. I was the only one who seemed to struggle with this inconsistency, however; no one else was surprised that I was back. Some said they thought I would never leave San Francisco. Others didn't think it was a big deal since the pandemic had created shifts in many people's lives. And it had been an easy return: When I made the decision to come back, one of my roommates was moving out to live with her boyfriend, so there was an open room in my own apartment for me to slide back into. Chloe, my friend who had moved in two years prior and whom I wanted to take over the lease, had said that as long as she was there, she'd always consider the place my home as well.

One of my reasons for coming back to San Francisco, one I didn't freely admit, was that I'd met someone.

The past few years had served as an opportunity for me to reclaim a sense of my deeper self, yet I still longed for partnership. Carter and I had connected online during one of my visits to the Bay Area early in the year, just as COVID was hitting China and then Italy. I was tired of all the online dating I'd done in the nine months I was in Southern California. Carter seemed serious, and I craved stability. That March, he called me every evening. I hadn't experienced that kind of consistency in my life before, and it was comforting. While he talked more than he listened, he was convincing, allowing me to believe that we might build something together, even as he insisted that he wouldn't be in a long-distance relationship.

I knew when I called him on my long drive back to the city and he didn't answer that something was off. He texted me at some point to tell me that he was at the beach with friends but would meet me later in the week.

I was upset with him for not coming to see me right when I arrived; after all, he was the one who'd convinced me to come back to the Bay Area so we could give our relationship a shot. I'd thought he'd be eager to see me, but I'd been wrong.

He'd once told me I was fragile and delicate. I didn't disagree.

By the time the anniversary of my mother's passing came around in late April, I only saw signs that he wouldn't be there for me. That's what I saw in most men, frankly. I never saw what they did, only what they didn't do, which was never a good starting point for a relationship.

He did see me one time that first week back, but when he opted to watch a sports event with friends instead of spending time with me over the weekend, I ended whatever it was that we had. Instead of talking to him, however, I sent a text message—just as I had done with the last man I'd dated.

That was my pattern, and one of the many reasons my relationships didn't last very long. A volcano of emotions often erupted at the beginning of my relationships—emotions I had buried beneath a tough exterior—and the intensity of those emotions frightened the men I dated, pushed them away. They scared me as well; I didn't know how to handle them any better than the guys did.

I was conscious of the fact that I hadn't properly dealt with all my emotions from my early life—specifically, my grief over losing my mother. It was always boiling underneath the surface. But I didn't know where or how to even begin to address what was going on within me.

✦✦

The first weekend I was back in town, I met my friend Chris at his mother's place in the East Bay. I told him about Carter—explained that he was why I'd returned to San Francisco, and that it wasn't working out.

Chris's mother, Estrella, had become somewhat of a mother figure to me over the years. I was embarrassed to tell her and others about yet another failed relationship. I was prone to feeling judged for making bad choices in dating, even if nothing was said aloud. I wanted more than anything to show them, and myself, that I could be in a sustainable relationship.

Rather than focusing on this most recent breakup, Chris nudged me to look at the bigger picture. "Christina," he said, "you really need to break this pattern. I don't know why you choose the men you do. Men who aren't there for you and aren't available for you."

"You're right," I acknowledged.

"You're always chasing this type of man," he continued. "This isn't any different from the other situations I've seen you in."

I knew he was concerned, but I felt the familiar clutch of failure in my stomach, in my heart. *I have to break this pattern*, I decided.

It was time to explore, address, and even conquer everything that was holding me back from being in a relationship. A good one. A real one. Not one that was fabricated in my mind. I also needed to figure out how to end the subconscious attraction I had to unavailable, distant men—men who in many ways mirrored my father.

The next day, when I thought about why the ending of this brief affair with Carter saddened me so much, I called Terra, whose wisdom and intuition I trusted.

She said it wasn't just about this man. "Every time something ends with a man, you feel a deeper wound, Christina. It's a yearning within you for someone to be there for you. You're living through all the disappointment once again. You're not the only woman who faces this challenge. Many women do."

Nothing about being back in San Francisco felt comfortable by that point. It wasn't just about my patterns in relationships. It was about being single and childless and newly forty, all of which gave me a lot to think about as I considered where I was going next, where I would call my future home. There was something in my body calling for change. A transformation was beckoning to me—and somehow I knew, deep in my bones, that it was one my current environment wouldn't be able to support.

One of the silver linings of being back in the Bay Area was living near David, one of my closest friends. He felt more like an older brother or a spiritual sibling than a mere friend. Sometimes I felt that my mother might have even had some role in bringing us together. We often joked that our lives were like parallel motorbikes: sometimes he was a bit ahead of me, sometimes I was a bit ahead of him, but we were on similar paths—paths that didn't look conventional from the outside.

We'd met through mutual friends in Vietnam. After living in Hanoi for six months, I'd decided to move to Saigon, and there happened to be a room open in David's house. It felt serendipitous—even more so after we learned that long before we met, his mother and my uncle had crossed paths.

Before moving to Vietnam, David's mother, Hương, who was originally from Central Vietnam but by then lived in New Jersey, sat next to my uncle, my mother's youngest brother, who lived in Saigon, on a flight. Hương took my uncle's information for David so they could connect when he arrived there.

I didn't even know I *had* an uncle in Vietnam when I first moved to Saigon. This information was only revealed to me once I got there. My Uncle Minh emailed me his younger brother's address, saying that I should try to stop by and see him. When my mother's family visited us in Indiana during her illness, no one had ever mentioned another family member still in Vietnam—so I was excited to meet this person, but also perplexed. Was he estranged from the family? Maybe this newfound uncle would be my key to learning more about Vietnam and my family in general, since my parents had spoken very little about their motherland during my childhood.

I went to my uncle's house and met his wife and son, and afterward excitedly returned home to tell David about my uncle Nam. "He owns some sort of fishing company, and he has a son named Ali. And he goes by Mohalam."

These names were quite unusual for Vietnamese people, and David's eyes widened.

"I think I've been to his house," he exclaimed. "I've met him before!"

Had it not been for my uncle's unusual name, we might not have made the connection. From that time forward, I felt that our friendship was somehow destined to be. What were the chances, after all, that David would meet my uncle in Saigon—a city of nearly nine million people—before me?

Our paths were undeniably similar, and this also bound us together. David and I had both worked for two different advertising agencies in Saigon; years later, we'd each found ourselves at international organizations in roles that involved planning and coordination of international conferences. While in the Bay Area, we'd both worked for universities.

Beyond our career paths, we'd also had similar relationship patterns, often grappling with our own emotional distance and unavailability. We both dated men, so there was a lot to share about the emotional turbulence we both confronted and seemed ill-equipped to handle in those relationships.

The Veil Between Two Worlds

Whenever people met David, they could see the ease and closeness of our friendship. On a visit to California, my aunt, who lives in Switzerland, even asked me why David couldn't be my boyfriend. But he was gay, of course—and regardless, we related to each other like siblings. He was one of the few friends I trusted with the entire truth about my family's history and dynamics, and who I felt could understand what was happening in my life on a deep level.

Given our history together, it wasn't surprising that David would play a role in my second departure from San Francisco and that my timing would coincide with his own need for a change.

When one of my downstairs neighbors informed me that she was moving out of her apartment and one of her roommates was looking for a place to land for six months before starting a new job and moving to the East Bay, I thought it was the universe opening up a six-month window for me to go.

It was the perfect situation: the downstairs neighbor could take over my place in the apartment, and I'd have more time to figure out where I'd land permanently.

Different thoughts ran through my head: *Maybe I'll drive cross-country. Maybe I'll go see my dad in Northern Virginia. I could visit friends and family along the way in Southern California, Arizona, Texas, Georgia, and North Carolina!*

When I mentioned this plan to a friend, she looked at me wide-eyed. "You can't leave," she said. "It's COVID. It's unsafe for a single Asian woman to travel cross-country alone. There are a lot of Trump supporters along that path."

She didn't get it, and I didn't want to share the deeper call of the journey with her. I'd learned from past mistakes that sharing with others could backfire, and that listening to the whisper was the only path to deeper fulfillment.

Our conversation did give me pause, however. I thought through the practicalities and considered the element of safety. Perhaps traveling solo the whole way wasn't a great idea. Maybe instead of driving cross-country, I'd fly to my dad's place and then rent a car and travel through the South.

I messaged David: *Do you want to borrow my car for a few months if I leave San Francisco?*

He'd coined my car—a white Honda HRV I had purchased for a floral business I'd run for four years, up until my first departure from San Francisco in 2019—the "sacred car." He'd used it once to transport plant medicine from Santa Cruz to the Bay Area and had told me afterward that he'd felt safe in it—that it had good energy. I felt similarly. In the nine months I'd spent away from San Francisco, my car had felt like the only stable thing in my life.

The next time David and I spoke, he asked me when I was thinking about leaving.

"Maybe January fifteenth," I said. That was two weeks away.

"I was literally just looking for a rental car for around that time," he said. "I'm going to a plant medicine ceremony that weekend. In Santa Barbara."

My ears perked up. A ceremony in Santa Barbara sounded perfect for me. I'd only been to two similar ceremonies before then—both of them with David, who had introduced me to the medicine and to this specific community.

"Do you think I can go too?" I asked.

"I don't see why not," he said. "Just check in with Saanvi to see if there's space."

I emailed Saanvi, whom I knew from the previous ceremonies. She was a friend and mentor to David, and the shaman hosting the ceremony. When she responded that yes, there was space, I proposed a road trip to David. When else would we have this opportunity to leave for a few months and explore together?

Doing this trip with David—not alone—felt like a first step toward the life I wanted to live: a life more connected to the lives of others. I knew what it meant to be independent; I'd spent most of my adult life flying solo. There were other lessons for me to learn now: what it meant to be independent and maintain a free-spirited nature and still be connected to others. And maybe there was a deeper discovery in store for me as well.

I packed two suitcases, my white down comforter, and a few extra bags. I had no idea when, or if, I would return to the Bay Area. The seeds of awareness had started to sprout for me a long time ago; deep within me, I knew that living in this unattached way wasn't all I'd once thought it to be. I understood there was a difference between running away from whatever it was I didn't want to face and running toward a future, a place, a life that held the promise of being more enriching, nourishing, and meaningful.

I hoped that this time around I was running toward something, not running away.

Chapter 2

Longing

David arrived at my apartment on a beautiful January day. The air was crisp, the sky was blue, and there was no fog rolling into the valley from Twin Peaks. It was the kind of day when I felt grateful to live in California, and it made me wonder why I was so desperate to leave San Francisco.

Nearly a decade had passed since I'd found my Noe Valley apartment, which I'd landed after attending an open house in the summer of 2011.

I was thirty-one and living in Vietnam when I felt the pressure to build something stable for myself—to forgo my nomadic existence and return to San Francisco to put down roots. Prior to that, all through my twenties, I'd been on the move. I'd ventured to Hanoi, and then to Saigon, right after college. I'd bounced around between graduate school in London, working in San Francisco for a year, spending time in Hanoi, then Geneva, and then Hanoi again. I couldn't stay in one place longer than two years. I'd moved so frequently throughout my life, even my childhood, that leaving seemed to be an integral part of my existence.

The Veil Between Two Worlds

Before I moved back to Noe Valley, my friends couldn't keep track of where I was living. Many often asked, "When are you going to settle down?" Some called my lifestyle "admirable" and "brave," but I knew that underlying those words was another thought—that I was afraid to commit to a place, to people, to anything like a home.

In Hanoi, before making my next move to San Francisco, I spent an entire year plotting and dreaming about what my life in the city would look like. I created inspiration boards to help envision the physical appearance of my ideal home—a typical San Francisco apartment in a charming neighborhood, walking distance from coffee shops and restaurants. I would have a tall, upholstered headboard in my bedroom with a fluffy white duvet, European shams, and vintage, white-painted furniture. I would create the look of a bedroom in a French country inn. In the living room, there'd be a white sofa with bold yellow-and-gray-patterned pillows. I'd find a local craftsman to build a wooden kitchen table. Most importantly, I imagined a home full of people—a home frequently graced by dinner parties and out-of-town guests. In addition to living among a rich community of friends, I wanted my home to be rooted in a physical structure, a safe abode. More than any desire to build a stable career or family, I was fixated on creating a true home for myself, since "home" had always been an elusive notion.

I immediately fell in love with the apartment, a three-bedroom with two common rooms located on the second floor of an Edwardian building. It was right on 24th Street, the main thoroughfare in Noe Valley, an area dotted with bars, restaurants, high-end boutiques, and a handful of nail salons. The turquoise building with purple awnings stood alone, with a public parking lot next door and a Wells Fargo branch on the other side. It seemed like a lonely building on a bustling thoroughfare in a quiet neighborhood. The apartment reminded me of myself—appearing strong and sturdy on the outside yet, upon closer inspection, in need of some TLC. I felt the apartment had a spirit, and it was kindred to mine.

At the open house, I waited for all the eager potential tenants to leave, then told the landlord, Linda, that I would pay one hundred dollars above her desired rent.

A few hours later, she called me and said, "I knew when you offered the extra money that you really wanted the place, and that you'd take care of it. It's yours."

David had also just moved to San Francisco after finishing graduate school in Boston, and it seemed predestined that we would share a place. I recruited a new friend, Melissa, to take the third room, and together we set about creating a home.

In my mind, home and its essence revolved around my mother.

As I remember her, she was always in the kitchen, cooking for us. Growing up, she would ask us every morning what we wanted to eat for dinner that night, and it would be ready on a plate on the kitchen table when we arrived home from school. At the time, I found it rather annoying to be asked about dinner so early in the morning—but as an adult, I can see how dedicated my mother was to making sure we ate homemade food every day. She made everything from fresh baguettes to roast chicken to Vietnamese dishes and almost all Asian cuisine in general. She was a creative cook, never afraid to try something new, even if she didn't get it right on the first try. She'd often make plates full of egg rolls so my father could bring them to the nurses at the hospital where he worked.

Not only was she a central figure because of the way she nourished us with her cooking, she was also our primary vessel of communication with our father, who spoke very little. If we had a question for him or wanted anything, we asked my mother, who would then talk to our father.

The home we shared that is most imprinted in my mind is the one we lived in when she died. We moved in when I was eleven, two years before she was diagnosed with cancer. That home, constructed by Amish builders, was located in The Woods, a neighborhood a fifteen-minute drive from Preston, a small Southern Indiana town with a population of around 13,000. When she died, our home felt unfinished, as though it had never had a chance to fully bloom—very much like my own mother.

Before her passing, we'd spent months carefully choosing the details of our future home—everything from the exterior bricks to the wood stain to the cabinets to the floors. Largely influenced by my father, I had grown up appreciating houses, both their structures and their contents. He often drove my sister and me to neighborhoods with large homes we could never afford, just to look. This created a sense of longing in me—a false belief that other homes, especially bigger ones, were better. As a kid, I used to pore over the floor plans of homes in *Southern Living* magazine at the grocery store checkout counter. We had moved so frequently, from Connecticut to Utah to Tennessee to Illinois to Indiana, that I didn't entirely understand what feeling "at home" meant.

The timing of my mother's death was unfortunate. It would have been devastating no matter when it happened, but it came right when our family was finally settling into a new home in Indiana, supposedly for good—right when I had begun to allow myself to believe in the possibility of a forever home. That dream was shattered by my mother's death.

For years after her passing and well into my adult life, I would struggle with that loss—with the mother wound. I understood at a visceral level what it was like to be a motherless daughter. I could see how her absence affected all my relationships, my ability to connect with people, and my own construction of a sense of home. But I'd worked with therapists and healers to address that wound; I'd explored the depth of it. By now, at forty, I had healed it.

Or so I believed.

That I'd been open enough to create some semblance of a home in my Noe Valley apartment was what made it most difficult to leave.

In the weeks before we moved in, the contractor, Brandon, put the finishing touches on the place. After asking permission from my landlord, I moved a few of my things in before the apartment was totally ready, so I met him a few times.

The first time, I was surprised that he was so handsome—at least six feet tall, with curly strawberry blond hair, bright blue eyes, and a rugged look that I found attractive.

He walked down the stairs to greet me. "I'm Brandon," he said. "Do you want some help with your bags?"

He wore a baseball cap and a white T-shirt printed with an image I recognized as Vietnamese on the front. It could have been purchased from any number of the touristy areas of Hanoi or Saigon.

"I lived in Vietnam!" I exclaimed. "I just moved back early in the year. Have you been?"

"No," he responded, "but a friend of mine bought this shirt for me on a recent trip. I would love to go one day."

As we did a walkthrough of the apartment, we exchanged stories. He told me that contracting work paid the bills, but he was really a musician. "I have a recording studio in the Mission," he added. "And once I shot photos for our album cover on these stairs. Don't tell Linda that."

What he said about his creative life resonated with me. "I'm working on a book," I shared, "about my family and their journey from Vietnam. But I doubt I will ever try to publish it, or even become a writer."

I changed the subject quickly after making that admission, embarrassed that I was only halfheartedly committing to my creative pursuits. I pivoted to pointing out everything in the apartment that I disliked.

"I don't like the colors of the rooms," I said.

Linda and I had actually joked that Brandon might be color-blind because the colors he chose—baby blue, sunny yellow, and a flat gray—didn't go together and weren't what she'd requested.

"I want to repaint all the rooms eventually," I told him, "but I'll start with painting my room white."

"You do realize that all these rooms have just been freshly painted," he said. "You're going to be repainting over what was just done."

It was hard to tell if he was annoyed or just stating facts.

"I know, but I can't live with these colors," I explained.

He gave me a look that conveyed frustration, but said, "Do whatever you want. It's your place now."

Seeming to get over it pretty quickly, he went on to tell me what horrible condition the place had been in before he started work on it. The previous tenant—a woman nicknamed Fluzi who'd lived there for about a decade—had painted the wood floors black. Brandon had to strip and restore them.

"Every room was rented to a tenant," he shared. "She had a deadbolt on her bedroom door. I imagine they all just lived in their rooms. This apartment needs a lot of love."

"I'll take care of it," I assured him. "I want to build a home for myself."

During those weeks, I started creating a nest for myself while Brandon was still working on the place. We bonded over our shared goal for the apartment to become a home. He told me about his own desire to have a family and a house in an area of Northern California where his parents lived.

I didn't have the same notion of home. I didn't need to have a family; I just wanted a stable place to live, a home where I felt safe.

Brandon gave me tips on how to paint, even though I was painting over his work. Sometimes we ate lunch together on the back patio; I'd buy a small deep-dish pizza from Patxi's across the street and bring it back to share. Once he went to Starbucks for an afternoon coffee and asked what I wanted. I requested a double espresso over ice, and when he returned, he handed me a small bag with a cake pop inside it in addition to my drink.

One day I arrived at the apartment and noticed three small houseplants next to the fireplace in the living room.

"Where did these come from?" I asked.

"It's a housewarming gift from me," he responded.

For the weeks that we overlapped in the Noe Valley apartment, as we nurtured the apartment into a livable home, it felt like I was building something with a partner—a shared experience I had yet to discover until this point. I would come to realize much later that sometimes we transfer our hopes and desires onto people without actually having feelings for them. I didn't have feelings for Brandon, but he represented something to me: the idea of building a home and creating a life with someone.

Something I thought I would one day do in the Noe Valley apartment, but never did.

Chapter 3

Loss

After we'd lived in the apartment for three weeks, Melissa, David, and I spent one morning discussing how to set up our living room with the white sofa we'd just purchased from IKEA. Melissa shared my love for decorating and had created a Pinterest board for her room that reminded me of something straight out of a West Elm catalog. David was relaxed and didn't have strong opinions about the aesthetics of the home. I'd started to buy new decor for the place—affordable items I found scouring through Craigslist and local flea markets—and things were coming together.

I baked two blueberry cobblers that morning: one to bring to a barbecue that David and I were attending that afternoon, the other for the three of us to share later.

When we arrived at the barbecue, I excitedly told our friends about how I was decorating the apartment. I also mentioned the date I was going on later that day with a man who lived in our neighborhood.

I checked my phone and noticed a text message from my date. Assuming it had to do with our plans for later that day, I was surprised to instead read a startling message: *Hey, I don't mean to alarm you but I think your apartment is on fire.*

After that, I received a flurry of texts from the upstairs neighbors, though the only word my eyes could fix on was "fire."

I grabbed David and told him we had to leave immediately. "I think our apartment is on fire."

As we dashed out, friends asked, "Is everything all right?"

"Christina thinks our place is on fire, but I think she's exaggerating," David said. He rolled his eyes, but he still followed me out.

A high school friend from Indiana, who now lived in San Francisco, jumped in the taxi with us to offer support. He called the Valley Tavern, the bar across the street from our building, to see if they knew anything.

When he got off the phone, he said, "It's definitely your building that caught fire."

Thoughts flooded my mind: *Was it my fault? Did I leave the stove on when I made the blueberry cobbler?*

When we arrived, firefighters and The Red Cross were already there. The cause of the fire was unknown, and they assured us they would let us know when we could return to the apartment to see what, if anything, was salvageable. Brandon was there as well; Linda had texted him. He told me he worried it was something he'd done that caused the fire.

The guy I was supposed to go out on a date with showed up too.

"I don't really know what to do in this situation," he said.

"I don't really know what I need," I told him.

"How about I go get a pie from Mission Pie? Maybe that would help a little?" he asked.

"Sure, that's fine," I told him, though the only thoughts running through my mind had to do with whether all the new furniture and decorations I'd bought over the past few weeks had survived.

The Veil Between Two Worlds

✦✦

During the nine months that my mother was living with cancer, she made every effort to maintain a sense of normalcy in the house—took great pains to conceal any signs that her body, or our home, was changing. Nonetheless, we faced daily reminders that our lives were in fact morphing drastically before our eyes. The potpourri pot sitting atop the kitchen counter, next to the telephone, still released its sweet, familiar fragrance, a floral scent I'd grown used to, but the kitchen shelves, which had formerly housed sugary cereals, cookies, and potato chips were now packed with small, shiny cans of a liquid called Ensure Plus, a nutritional supplement that helped keep my mother from losing too much weight, and the space beneath our TV stand was now stocked with medical supplies—syringes, cleansing wipes, rubber gloves.

My father took care of her, silently. He warmed the heating pad for her in the middle of the night when the pain in her hip became too sharp to tolerate and she was barely able to lift her leg. After he returned home from work, he'd take her on long drives, just to get her out of the house. I've tried to imagine how those drives must have felt for both of them; what they spoke about as they drove past the soft, rolling hills of Southern Indiana; if they ever broached the topic of what life would be like for us without her. I've wondered if my mother offered my father any advice for the future, for taking care of two teenage daughters who would soon become his sole responsibility.

Somehow my mother still found the wherewithal to cook, except for the few nights of the week when my father would bring home Chinese takeout or Kentucky Fried Chicken—foods we had rarely eaten before my mother's diagnosis. Those days we knew, without being told, that our mother was too tired or sick to cook for us.

My parents slept in the same bedroom, which they hadn't done for much of my childhood, but they slept in separate beds—my mother on a queen-size bed in the center of the room, my father on a twin bed he'd placed beside the window. He must have heard her whimpers of pain in the middle of the night and must have responded however he was able. I was never sure how her sickness and suffering affected him, to be truthful—whether he was used to dealing with sick patients because he was a doctor, or whether it was different for him caring for my mother, his own wife, as a patient. His face never betrayed any emotion, and I intuitively knew that I wasn't supposed to ask.

I walked into their room once when my mother was adjusting the bag that had to be attached to her abdomen after the colonoscopy. I couldn't bear it—looking at the plastic bag that stored her excess waste, the protrusion from her body so stark and unnatural. I backed out of the room quickly, trying to forget what I'd seen, vaguely nauseated—with shame for her, for all of us, for myself and my own repulsion.

She still woke up early, though she was getting sicker and sicker. She'd heat up a baguette, one she'd made from scratch and kept frozen in the freezer, and spread it with pâté for my father, her version of a Vietnamese sandwich. Then she'd spray the kitchen counter with Windex and wipe the kitchen sink, as she always had, so there were no visible drops of water. By the time I came downstairs, she had already exhausted herself, and I'd find her napping on the paisley couch. Her broken black rosary would be wrapped around her hand, her pocket-size green Bible on the coffee table.

Sometimes I arose early and pretended, for her sake, that I, too, was reading a Bible. I'd heard her once on the phone telling one of her best friends about how good I was because I prayed with her in the morning before school. She didn't know that even in those last months, I still wanted to secure her affection and affirmation—anything to prove to myself that I was indeed a good daughter.

The Veil Between Two Worlds

My mother no longer resembled the slightly plump Vietnamese woman I'd grown up with. Her face was gaunt, her clothes–especially her pants–hung from her body, just like the skin that now seemed to hang from her fragile bones. She abandoned the fancy clothing she'd formerly preferred, which no longer fit her, choosing instead to wear the same baggy pink-and-orange floral pants with elastic on the front, because they didn't put too much pressure on the colostomy bag.

"I only wish that I had fat on my body again like you," she said to me one morning as she pinched the fat on my arms. "When I die, I'm afraid your father is going to marry an American woman. Maybe one of the nurses at the hospital."

She said this in a calm voice but I sensed her insecurity, her bittersweet and conflicting desire both for her husband's life to continue and to be reassured by her teenage daughter that life would *not* go on, that another woman could not possibly take her place as wife and mother.

"I don't think that will happen," I said. "I can't imagine Dad with an American woman."

But she carried on as if she hadn't heard me and believed the storyline had already been written. "Then you and Teresa will have to eat American food at American restaurants," she continued quietly, "when you have a new American mother."

My mother was wrong about the story she'd created in her mind about this future partner my father might have. He would remarry, but not to an American woman. Soon after my mom passed, he would begin dating a Vietnamese woman, Liên, who would eventually become our stepmother.

The day after the fire, we returned to the apartment to sift through the debris. Most of the damage had been in the upstairs unit. The four tenants who lived there had lost everything. The firefighters informed us that the stairs had caught fire when a burst of wind fanned something unspecified into a flame. We suspected a cigarette butt, but that was never confirmed.

Melissa, David, and I were the lucky ones. With the exception of our kitchen and living room, most of our personal items had been spared.

Slowly, we brought our belongings downstairs and placed them around a bench in the parking lot next door to our building. We didn't know where we would store our stuff. A passerby thought we were having a garage sale and asked if one of my small mirrors was for sale.

"We just had an apartment fire," I said. Over the next hour I had to repeat myself more than once, and was frustrated each time by the fact that people couldn't see that our building had burned.

I stuffed my emotions beneath the surface and focused on the task at hand: finding a place to store our belonging and a temporary place to stay. After making a few calls, we found a solution. A friend's brother-in-law who owned a house in Noe Valley offered to let us store our things in his garage and stay at his place since he was out of town for a few weeks.

A few days later, a neighborhood association launched a fundraiser for us, "The Noe Valley Fire Victims." They opened an account for each of our apartments at the Wells Fargo next door to our building. Neighborhood stores wrote to us, suggesting we come by and pick out something for free.

Between the two units, seven of us were displaced. One person went to stay with a friend, while the rest of us created a unit, albeit a dysfunctional one. Local real estate agents informed us of available apartments for rent for fire victims. Through Craigslist, we found a large house—a small mansion, really—with six bedrooms in the Castro. The homeowner ran a construction company and his plan was to work on the house and eventually flip it. He was willing to let us all move in if we agreed that he could stay in the basement unit.

I thought his home was perfect, and his name was Lynn, like my mother. I couldn't imagine a more suitable person to become our landlord. It was another moment where I believed that my mother was having a hand in my life from beyond.

While our new house felt like a luxurious space, none of us was fully prepared to live with five other people, especially as we each grappled with the trauma of being displaced from the fire. I couldn't deal with the underlying emotions of the experience, or really any of my emotions, so I did what I normally did: I stuffed my feelings beneath the surface and became laser-focused on tasks and building a life in my new space. A friend who'd shown up at the fundraiser told our mutual friend afterward that she'd felt dismissed by me, but I didn't have the bandwidth to be social. We were dealing with the weight of impermanence, and needing to find a home.

The fire fractured my relationship with David, who didn't appreciate the way my "bulldozer" personality had come to the surface during that time. We often butted heads. I felt he was too slow and methodical in his decision-making, and he believed I was too quick to reach conclusions and decisions. He criticized me for making choices for others without getting their consent—like when I told Melissa, who was out of town when we found our place in the Castro, that we "needed" her to live there rather than asked her for her opinion. In Vietnam, he'd named this side of my personality "Eileen," after the mean character in the movie *Monster*.

At the time of the fire, I'd just started looking for full-time work, since the consulting contract I'd had up to that point was coming to an end. A month prior, I'd applied for a position as a donor relations writer at the University of California, San Francisco. After we were displaced, I wrote a blog post for *The Noe Valley Voice,* a monthly neighborhood newspaper, about the fire and how it had damaged the beginnings of the home I longed to create in the neighborhood. The hiring manager, who coincidentally lived in Noe Valley, read the post, remembered my name from the application, and sent me an email asking if I was still looking for a job. She wrote that she was moved by my writing.

That's how an apartment fire landed me a job that I would end up staying in for the next four years.

Eileen in *Monster* was a very fitting comparison for the assertive side of my personality. I knew that I could come off as having a strong personality, but I didn't know how I felt about it. One of the defining aspects of my life had always been that my father didn't speak. Left with a silent parent after my mother's passing, I felt that I had to fill the voids and decipher what my father was thinking and express it for him.

As an adult, whenever anyone asked me about my father, this was the tidbit I offered.

"How could your father not speak?" a friend once questioned.

I'd often thought to myself, *How can anyone who hasn't lost their mother understand that loss?* And, similarly, *How can you understand a silent father if you didn't have one?*

David didn't believe me, initially, when I told him my father didn't speak—not until one afternoon when I still lived in Vietnam and David was there for his graduate school research. We were walking along the streets of Saigon in District 1, close to Notre Dame Cathedral, and he saw a friend—a Vietnamese American woman from the Midwest who was living in Saigon doing research for a film project—sitting inside a coffee shop.

She invited us to join her group. As we went around the table and made introductions, I noticed another young Vietnamese American man, around our age, sitting with an older man who I assumed was his father.

The Veil Between Two Worlds

When I mentioned that I was from Indiana and that my family still lived there, the older man looked curious.

"Oh, where are you from in Indiana?" he asked.

"Preston," I responded. "It's a small town about twenty miles south of Bloomington."

"We are from Indiana too," the older man said. "I am a professor at Indiana University. What's your surname?"

"Vo," I said.

"I think I know your sister," the son said. "She lived in my dorm."

"Wait," the father interjected, "I know your dad! He's the handsome Vietnamese man who doesn't talk."

"Yes, that's him," I said. "The man who doesn't talk."

When we left the café, David looked at me. "Wow, your father is actually known in Southern Indiana as the Vietnamese man who doesn't talk?"

"I've been telling you that for years," I said.

Having my father's silence noticed by another person made me feel validated. I breathed a sigh of relief at the realization that this truth had been seen by someone outside of my family.

Another aspect of my father's personality, however, was that when he decided to speak in depth, which was rare, he spoke so eloquently and thoughtfully that it was shocking.

I experienced one of these rare moments as a twenty-year-old college student when I attended a Saigon Medical School reunion in Falls Church, Virginia, with my father. It took place at a rather opulent home the owners called the "White House." I could see how proud they were of the lives they'd created in America, and that the large home they constructed was a symbol of that success.

That day, in front of all his classmates and their families, my father stood up and shared a story called "The Pilgrims," in which he detailed his own journey, and that of many of the other guests at the event, rebuilding their lives and careers from the fragments of the war they'd left behind after moving from Vietnam to the United States. I was amazed by the power of his words, and that so many complex thoughts and emotions lay beneath the surface of his quiet disposition.

At my mother's funeral, he spoke beautifully—poetically, even—about her life, and shared many details about her and their life together that I didn't even know myself. I will never forget the shocked looks I saw on the faces of my friends and classmates, who had never heard my father speak, as he gave his heartwarming testament to the woman he'd loved that day.

But other than those few times, my father was simply a man who didn't speak, or at least chose not to converse with his family—and this truth followed me throughout my life like a shadow. Even at forty, I often felt paralyzed when trying to find my voice, which sometimes became a problem with the men I dated. I didn't know how to speak my truth to men because, well, I hadn't ever learned how to speak to my father.

While the fire opened a lot of new possibilities for me that I couldn't have predicted, it had the effect of creating distance between me and David.

A year after the fire, when the apartment was finally rebuilt, I was the only tenant who returned. The five others had already found new permanent homes and moved on. Linda offered me first choice between the apartments, so I chose the top unit—the one that had sustained the most damage and hence was the most renovated of the two. The apartment, like me, was starting afresh after the fire.

Returning to that building felt like the real beginning to my San Francisco life. Now, finally, I would be able to nest and build the home in San Francisco I so desired. My spirit and the spirit of the building felt intertwined, just as they had been when I first moved in. The apartment needed a caretaker, and I needed a home. We were a perfect match. Here, I would work through so many wounds around home and being motherless. Through my relationships with housemates, I could witness, and fix, the overbearing parts of myself that wanted to fix and save others—to give to them what I felt I had not received myself. It was the place where I would live long enough to finally address, and ultimately heal, the mother wound . . . or so I thought.

Over the years, David and I saw each other less and less. We would run into each other at gatherings and were always friendly to one another, but there was a noticeable distance between us. For a few years, he lived just a few streets away, and yet we rarely made time to see one another. We were both living our San Francisco lives. I got into a long-term relationship that would last for four years, and though I knew David supported the relationship and believed having stability was vital for me, he kept his distance. Our lives were running in parallel; our paths sometimes crossed, but we weren't connected. I wasn't tapped into my emotions enough at that time to acknowledge how much I missed, and likely needed, our friendship during those years.

Chapter 4

Grandmother

B y the time our paths realigned again—eight years after the fire, and two years before the road trip journey neither of us had any idea was on the horizon—David and I were in similar places . . . again. We were each in the midst of deeper spiritual changes. Tired of the mundane. Weary of our jobs (though for me this was more existential, and I attributed a lot of what I was feeling to being in San Francisco specifically). We were both on the brink of deeper changes in our lives—awakenings, on some level.

It surprised me when we spoke how aligned I felt with him once again, and yet it made sense to me, too. After all, we were on parallel motorbikes.

David had been exploring sitting in ayahuasca ceremonies and using plant medicines to delve deeper into the ancestral and familial wounds he'd brought into this life. He sat regularly, for about a year, with a community led by Saanvi and formed specifically for people of color and those racialized as white who were working to unravel how systemic racism and being a person of color affected their lives and their emotional well-being, as well as all the other forms of trauma a person endures in their lifetime.

For a long time, I shied away from participating in any form of spiritual community—until I met Terra at a meditation center in San Francisco. In her I found a spiritual teacher, and we quickly became close. She was in her early fifties, had the most lovely English accent, and exuded a wonderful maternal energy. I felt a connection not only to her but also to the women's work that she was beginning.

When we met for the first time during a shamanic journey she was leading, she came up to me and whispered into my ear, "You have so much creative energy that's ready to come through you. You think it comes through your head, but it actually starts in your womb. From the place where all women give birth."

I felt she could see right through me, could read me perfectly. She was right: I was overthinking my creative projects. Creativity didn't just encompass art projects and specific creative endeavors. To me, it referred to how I wanted to live my life: I believed there was a deeply spiritual element to creativity.

Coincidentally, Terra and Saanvi knew each other. They'd been part of the same spiritual community in the East Bay and often sat in ceremonies together before they had a falling-out over some incident related to a Peruvian medicine woman. I thought it was another sign of the parallel between my life and David's—that we had both met spiritual teachers around the same time who were connected to one another.

So when David invited me to attend an ayahuasca ceremony in Berkeley with him in early 2019, after we'd had so much distance in our friendship, I felt this marked a return to a former closeness that I was missing. I'd be turning forty that October. The time was ripe to bring new experiences into my life.

He extended the invitation by saying, "Going to this ceremony would be good for you. You never know what you'll uncover."

I felt every bone in my body say "yes" to this novel experience. Anything that would help shift my life out of its current configuration sounded like a good idea to me.

I didn't know what to expect from my first ayahuasca ceremony. All I knew about plant ceremonies I'd heard from people who'd gone to South America, and then, more recently, from David, who shared his experiences of sitting regularly in the community he had joined. He explained to me that ayahuasca was known to the indigenous of the Peruvian Amazon as *Abuela*–Grandmother. She was often referred to as the sentient mother spirit of nature, and many believed that ingesting her medicine made it possible for a person to receive the healing and teachings from Grandmother herself.

The week before the ceremony, I diligently followed the guidelines, including the restrictions on diet set forth by the community. Limiting our intake of processed foods, meat, seafood, coffee, sugar, and dairy products would apparently help prepare our bodies, minds, and spirits for this specific healing work. Whatever I was getting ready to embark on, I took it seriously.

David helped me, too, by telling me what the setup would look like for the two-day ceremony and advising me on what to pack. I took Friday afternoon off work, gladly escaping the routine of my job. Fear and excitement ran through my body, and in my typical fashion, I couldn't help but tell everyone I knew about what I was about to do–my way of easing my nervousness.

A few weeks prior to the ceremony, I had dinner with four of my closest friends. When I told them about the ceremony, they dismissed the whole thing as silly.

They were two couples–pairs of doctors and lawyers married to one another. Anh-Thu had been my closest female friend and confidante over the previous seven years, but we'd been drifting apart.

The Veil Between Two Worlds

Although I still joined her and her partner, Craig, for what felt like family Sunday dinners in their Berkeley townhouse at least twice a month, I'd witnessed a distinct shift in our friendship in recent months. It saddened me, though I understood it was a result of the ways our lives were diverging. They now had a toddler to attend to. The other couple, Luis and Elizabeth, were also trying to start a family.

"What!" Anh-Thu exclaimed when I brought up my impending trip. "Why are you going to do that?"

Luis, one of the lawyers, chimed in with his sarcastic humor, "So, you're going to sit in a dark room and listen to people purge all night? What's the point of that?"

"Do you have to pay for it?" Craig asked.

I didn't want to answer their questions, and I felt embarrassed that I'd even brought it up. *This ceremony felt important to me*, I wanted to tell them. As important as whatever was happening in their lives. But they were focused on their coupled lives. They didn't have time for the inner exploration I was embarking on, and I didn't feel they could understand what I was doing.

I looked down at my plate, holding back tears. I wanted them to ask deeper questions: *Why are you going? What are you seeking?* But I knew they wouldn't want to engage in that way, so instead I changed the subject.

"We should plan another getaway for the next holiday," I offered. "Maybe Presidents' Day weekend."

A weekend excursion would be something we could all bond over, rather than continuing to try to make them understand why I wanted to attend an ayahuasca ceremony.

It wasn't just those four friends I felt I was growing away from. It was many of my friends in the Bay Area. I didn't know it then, but this ceremony, and the deeper spiritual path I would subsequently embark upon, would end up creating a rift in some of my closest friendships. I wanted to experience something beyond my normal day-to-day existence, but many of my friends simply wanted to adhere to the status quo. It was something I would have to reconcile myself with.

In some ways, though, I couldn't blame them for failing to understand. I was venturing down another path that was unclear even to me—so how could I explain it to anyone else?

My spiritual journey emerged from a desire to connect, to find something deeper and more meaningful. I had regrets about the lack of connection in my family life, for the ways in which my father and sister and I had failed to be a family after my mom died. I wished I had a strong sense of a nuclear family, but I didn't. I also wasn't creating a family of my own, which begged the question: where would I find that deeper sense of connection and belonging if not from a family unit?

Of all the roles I had tried to fulfill in my nearly four decades of life, I hadn't become the sister, aunt, and daughter I'd imagined. Growing up, my sister and I had never been close. The loss of our mother and our formative childhood years bonded us, but we couldn't have been more different. I was extroverted, bubbly, and fearless, while Teresa was reserved, shy, and timid. I was popular and always in the mix; my sister floated along the periphery, and although she demonstrated more heart and tenderness than me, she didn't allow many people to see her true self.

I carefully watched her throughout our childhood, seeing the impact of our move from Illinois to Indiana when she was in eighth grade and I was in sixth. Being uprooted as a teenager to begin a new life in a small Indiana town right before high school wasn't easy for her. The wilder side of her personality, though, had already begun to emerge in Illinois—sneaking out of the house on the weekends, picking fights with a boy from her class. While I hoped it was just a rebellious phase, it wasn't. In Indiana, she grew more distant and despondent. She didn't feel she fit in. Once she started driving, she spent her spare time working at Burger King, where she befriended a group of people I didn't like and met the man she would marry a few years later.

After my mother's death, my father made an appointment with the psychiatrist at the hospital where he worked. I felt so distant from the middle-aged man with a mustache and cheap suit sitting in front of me. He didn't know how to interact with us. He said it seemed we might be depressed and offered a prescription for my sister.

I avoided my family after my mom died, but I avoided myself too. On the surface, I was immersed in school and friends, graduating as valedictorian and class president. But beneath the good-girl exterior, I sought to fill voids, just like Teresa; I just did it through seeking attention from boys.

A few months after my mom died, I started dating a guy who was four years older than me. More than anything, I wanted to be part of his family. His family lived in town in a charming, picture-perfect house with a white picket fence. His parents were high school sweethearts, the homecoming queen and captain of the football team. Their home symbolized a heartfelt Americana that I thought would be nourishing. They attended church as a family every Sunday, then went to the grandparents' home for a huge lunch. I longed for what they had, but spending time with them wasn't the salve I thought it would be. At fourteen, my emotional voids were so large that they couldn't be satiated by one man or one family.

In later years, I would regret how things had played out with my sister—that I hadn't managed to save her, that I'd failed her.

Not only did this weigh heavily on my heart, it impacted the way I showed up for others in my adult life. I wanted to be the savior, even if I hadn't been asked. I was drawn to friendships with psychologically complex individuals, often resulting in unhealthy dynamics. I became a problem-solver and coordinator, the person upon whom others relied to get things done. While I resented this role, that's also where I felt most comfortable. I felt close to those I could help, but also to people, especially women, whom I perceived as being stronger than me.

A deeper truth was that I longed to have an older sister who wasn't numbing herself, who could be present for me. And I longed to have what I'd lost: the mother I could never get back, the family connection that had been fractured when she died.

We traveled only twenty miles over the Bay Bridge from San Francisco to Oakland, yet I felt my spirit was embarking on a grand adventure.

David told me that the Grandmother spirit of ayahuasca often begins even before one physically arrives at the ceremony. He said prior to the ceremony, things might happen that would illuminate some of the issues I might work through during the ceremony. It all felt so otherworldly.

When we pulled up to the giant Tudor house, it was as if we'd arrived in a magical land. The home itself reminded me of my father; he loved the Tudor style and had attempted to emulate it when we built our house in Southern Indiana.

A handful of people were in front, unloading their bags. They seemed to know the drill. I got the distinct feeling that I might be the only first-timer in attendance.

Inside the house, people who seemed to be assistants were busy moving and covering the furniture, the windows, and the fireplace in what would become the ceremonial room. David walked around to find a space that felt comfortable for him. I asked him how many people would be there.

"I don't know," he responded. "This one might be a big one.

Seems like at least twenty or twenty-five people." As he set up his space, he added, "You know, we can't talk during the ceremony so we don't interfere with each other's experiences. I know you like to share a lot, but we can talk more tomorrow morning, after the first ceremony is over."

David knew his role in my life well. He was a big brother to me. He knew my history, and more than any other person, he knew my wounds. He'd even once said to me that he felt the energy of my brother who had passed away as a toddler in Vietnam. *Maybe that's the role I'm meant to have in your life*, he said at the time. But I knew he was often overwhelmed by this role he hadn't asked for, and I believed it was one of the reasons he sometimes kept his distance from me.

The ceremonial room began to fill up as people set up their Back Jacks, fold-out sleeping pads, colorful blankets, even their altars. I felt wholly unprepared with my sleeping bag, pillow, and the white-and-gray-knit throw blanket that I'd grabbed from my couch at the last minute. I also, surprisingly, felt I wasn't stylish enough for the ceremony. Others seemed to have the attire down, when I hadn't even known there *was* one until now. People were dressed in indigenous prints, beaded jewelry, and other ceremonial-looking items. The gathering felt celebratory, and I watched, feeling increasingly alienated, as people who seemed to know each other greeted one another warmly.

The handful of people I interacted with were all friendly. There was an energy of deep reverence for what was about to unfold. I imagined each person was there because, like me, they were on a healing journey, exploring an aspect of their life that needed more attention. I questioned if my desire for a complete life shake-up was too much, but I tried to quell my self-doubt.

Saanvi entered the room and sat at the head of the circle with a beautiful altar in front of her. She was an attractive Asian Indian woman with large brown eyes and dark hair that fell just beneath her shoulders. When I saw her, I didn't focus much on her appearance; rather, it was the strength and confidence of her overall presence that made an impact on me. I turned my attention to one of the assistants sitting next to her: an attractive Asian woman who looked to be in her late twenties. She wore a trendy, geometric-patterned poncho, leggings, a long necklace, and feather earrings. Even her setup for the overnight ceremony could have been an Instagram post of some stylish spiritual retreat that would attract people, specifically women, seeking spiritual clarity and enlightenment. I felt as if I had pitched a tent, while Saanvi's assistant was full-out glamping.

When I asked David about her, he told me her name was Destiny. "She has this incredible maternal wisdom," he said. "I think she had kids pretty young. You'll feel her energy during the ceremony."

She appeared youthful, yet she carried herself impressively in space. I saw in her that maternal energy David referenced and felt a tinge of jealousy surface within me.

Destiny stood up, left the room, and came back with flowers. She had a presence to her that was nearly mesmerizing.

"My husband and kids just came over to bring these to me for the ceremony," she shared.

I was envious that her family cared so much about her spiritual experience that they'd brought her flowers. I hadn't shared any of my spiritual journey with my father or my sister. I didn't have that kind of love and support in my life, and it was exactly what I was yearning for—precisely the deeper connection I so desired.

I believe part of our healing journey is our own, but we also carry within us a responsibility to heal the wounds of our ancestors. For me, the disconnection I felt within my family was not simply a wound that I carried in this lifetime but was an intergenerational wound that my mother suffered from as well.

The Veil Between Two Worlds

Prior to her cancer diagnosis, I wasn't even aware that my mother had a family outside of us. She never spoke of her parents or her siblings. She never talked about her history. She didn't even explain to us that she was Vietnamese but had been born and raised in Cambodia. To me, she didn't have a past. She was an island unto herself, even as she was the axis around which our family orbited.

During the time she suffered from cancer, her family members began to visit us—first my grandmother, and then my aunts and uncles. It was a miracle to me that she was being reunited with her family after being estranged from them all for nearly two decades (for reasons I, of course, was not privy to). The timing, when she had only eight months to live, was certainly serendipitous.

It started when my mother's older brother, Uncle Minh, who lived in Lafayette, Louisiana, and had been trying to find a way to reunite with my mother and our family, asked one of his Vietnamese friends if he knew of a pharmacist named Tung Vo—my father's brother who lived in New Orleans. The friend asked for a day or two to find his information. A few days later, the friend called my uncle Minh and left him a voicemail with my uncle Tung's phone number. If Uncle Minh hadn't asked for Uncle Tung's phone number, I'm not sure if my mother would have been reconnected with her family before her death.

My grandmother—a rather chilly woman, not at all the warm and doting grandmother I had hoped for—visited with my aunt Odette, my mother's eldest sister, and her partner from Paris. My mother's younger sister, Aunt Aline, and her two young children visited from Switzerland. Uncle Minh and his wife were the connectors who were in regular contact with my mother, offering much-needed nurturing and love during those few months.

One day while Aunt Odette was visiting, my sister and I came home from school to find the women gathered in the kitchen. Every inch of our kitchen table was covered with food—mainly Vietnamese dishes that seemed more authentic than what I was accustomed to, but also pound cake and brownies brought over by neighbors and my mother's two French friends who'd taught my mother to crochet and whom she'd invited over so my aunts would feel more comfortable, French speakers that they were. The scents of my uncle Gerard's specialty, *thịt kho,* a Vietnamese caramelized pork dish, lingered in the air.

The women's loud voices competed with each other as they nudged plates of food in front of each other, encouraging others to eat but careful not to take bites themselves. I pulled up a chair quietly, seemingly invisible, to listen to the stories they told, trying to piece together the clues to my mother's unknown past. The women created the extended web of relationships I had longed for, and in their company I felt a circle completed—for my mother, and also for me.

Odette was the eldest and therefore the family's matriarch, more so than my grandmother. Physically, she resembled my grandmother, with the same strong features—tall forehead, broad lips, carefully coiffed hair. But unlike my grandmother, she exuded warmth. She squeezed our faces and screamed our names—"Teresa, Tina!"—as she planted two warm kisses on our cheeks. She inquired daily during the duration of her visit about our level of French and reminded us constantly that we could come stay with her in France whenever we wanted to. She wore a kind expression that was drastically different from my grandmother's perpetual frown.

Aunt Odette dressed simply, in dark blue trousers that seemed too baggy for her and a silk top with a button-up V-neck cardigan. She smiled at me and my sister regardless of what we said or did, interjecting verbal affirmations so uncommon in our nuclear family—"My nieces. I finally get to see you. I love you so much." I did not know whether she actually felt love for us, but I thrived on her attention and relished her doting nature. I wondered, because I'd had so few encounters with aunts at that time, if they automatically loved their nieces, even if they did not really know them.

Laughter reverberated throughout the house during those family visits. It was a stark contrast to what home normally felt like when it was solely inhabited by the four of us. There was a fullness that I had never before experienced. And yet it was ephemeral, short-lived; within a matter of months, my mother was gone, and the visits stopped.

Chapter 5

Layers

The first night of the ceremony, my experience seemed light. I didn't feel much, actually. Saanvi had advised those of us who were newcomers to only take a small amount of the plant medicine, to see what kind of impact it had. I sat there most of the evening thinking that nothing was happening and waiting for the ceremony to be over. Toward the end, people brought out musical instruments and began to play and sing songs, and it was beautiful—but it felt more like a show, a celebratory event, than a spiritual experience.

I was able to recognize that perhaps part of a spiritual experience was joy—something I was, perhaps, denying myself—but even so, I told David the next morning that I felt I didn't want to stay another night.

"I kinda want to leave; I'm craving a rotisserie chicken," I joked. But then I expressed what was really going on: "Nothing really happened."

"Just wait," he assured me. "The medicine will show you what you need to see."

I didn't know then that when you're in the ceremonial space, what might seem irrelevant is actually part of the experience, a first step toward the deeper lessons that need to be unearthed. My desire to leave, to escape, was exactly what I needed to sit with, to examine.

The second evening, I felt overwhelmed. The medicine felt stronger. The room was darker. I could hear people crying, moaning, and going through their own experiences around me. I wanted to reach out to comfort those who were suffering, yet I saw that by focusing on others, I was resisting my own experience. I didn't want to be in the room anymore. It was too intense. I remembered that David told me we could ask the assistants for help—yet a fear arose in me around that as well. I didn't like to ask for help. In fact, I never asked for help.

When I finally drummed up the courage to ask for support, I couldn't make out the figure who walked past me; I simply reached out. "Help—I need help," I said as I grabbed hold of the person walking by.

When I stood up, I saw that it was Destiny, and she had her hand on the back of another person she was assisting.

"Come with us," she said, her voice comforting, "I'll find some-one else to help you while I'm with him."

As we walked out, she asked me what was wrong.

"It's too much for me," I said. "That room . . . It feels too heavy."

"What feels heavy?" she asked.

"Whatever I felt in there. The energy."

"Whatever is in there is inside of you as well," she responded.

We ended up in a small side room we were using as a storage area for people's belongings. Destiny and the guy she was assisting sat on the floor while I lay down on the one couch in the room.

One of the effects of the medicine I was experiencing was that everything and everyone around me changed forms. Suddenly, the man on the floor became my mother and Destiny was hovering over her, talking to her. The entire room was altered visually. I saw my mother crying into her two hands, full of fear, as Destiny tried to console her.

I interrupted their conversation and asked Destiny again to help me. I didn't feel like crying, but I was overwhelmed by the experience.

"Hold on," she said, "I'm going to find someone to stay here with him."

Once she'd found someone to take over for her, she led me outside to the area where there was a sacred fire.

"What are you scared of?" she asked. "Can you explain what's happening?"

"I don't know," I said. "It's a fear of being alone. It's a fear of staying in one place. It's a fear of asking for help."

"I think you're suffering from the mother wound," she said.

You don't know what you're talking about, I thought. She had no idea how much healing I'd done in relation to losing my mother. I suffered from many wounds, but the mother wound was not one of them.

I sidestepped her comment and started talking to her about sisterhood. "Isn't it great when women support each other? We need that in the world today."

I knew I wasn't in my truth as I spoke. I was avoiding what she was saying by changing the subject.

Unnerved, I broke from her even though I wanted to be with her; I moved to be with a group of people who were standing outside, and Destiny returned to the man she'd been assisting.

There was another man in the group, Công, who was also a helper. I grabbed hold of him and his form shape-shifted immediately. He became a younger version of my father.

"What's happening here?" a woman's voice asked—and suddenly I was in the presence of Saanvi. I felt like a child, clutching my father's arm.

"I need to stay here," I told her, "with Công."

"No," she said, "you need to go inside. You need to pray. You need to look at what's going on here. Pray like your life depends on it. Because it does."

"No," I said adamantly.

"This is important, Christina," she said sternly. "You need to pray."

I obeyed and went back inside, fear inside of me, although I didn't know what I was scared of, exactly.

I went back to my spot in the circle, right next to David. I surrendered to the medicine, whatever it wanted to show me. When I did, the powerful white light that filled the room changed shape and form: the voice of the energy turned calm and soothing, and more powerful than anything I'd ever experienced.

"We all have the power to create."

It was a woman's voice. The energy was female.

"Create beauty and whatever you want in the world," she said. "Creation, in all forms–this is why we are here."

I wanted to be enveloped in that energy for as long as possible. But the room suddenly shifted away from the white light, and an overwhelming feeling of separation opened up inside of me. A friend appeared before me, and I didn't know why. Suddenly I was in tears, bawling in a way I had never cried before. I felt separate from this male friend in particular, but also from men in general.

The ceremony was coming to an end. People were up dancing and singing, and once again there was a vibe of celebration. But I was still curled up in a ball, releasing emotions.

I didn't know what had happened, what I had uncovered. Was it the mother wound I was suffering from, as Destiny had suggested?

I'd identified as being "motherless" since the age of fourteen. In my twenties, the void had presented itself in my life as a sadness I didn't understand, an emptiness I couldn't pinpoint. In my thirties, I'd tried to fill this emptiness by creating stability—in a city, job, relationship, apartment. But that approach had only left me feeling dead inside.

As I approached my forties, I'd finally begun to feel some deeper level of understanding of my mother's life and the impact of her death on me, recognizing that the pain I'd been left with was interconnected with my relationship with my father and my sister. But I also thought that by now I'd grown accustomed to the fact of my loss. Yes, at every significant moment, I was reminded that I didn't have a mother to call to celebrate the big victories or to cry to when I was heartbroken. Still, I believed I had healed from those wounds.

During the time of this ceremony, I didn't grasp that I was sitting at a threshold. In three months, I would be honoring the twenty-fifth anniversary of my mother's death; in nine months, I would turn forty. Both milestones were significant. So many questions about my life were beginning to surface: How did I feel about being single and childless at forty? Was it a decision I'd consciously made, or had I not had a family only because the right person hadn't come along? How did I really feel about my life in San Francisco and who I had become?

Lately, I'd felt my mother's presence in my life more strongly than ever before. She'd always been there for me, ever since her passing in 1994, gently supporting me in my decisions and helping me navigate my course, but this year in particular I needed her presence, guidance, and love. I needed her to journey with me as I reconciled my womanhood, my choices, my relationship with my family, and my understanding of myself.

I imagined the overwhelming sadness and separation that had appeared during the ceremony had to do with loss, but I didn't know what to do with all of it, where to put it.

The Veil Between Two Worlds

✦✦

The next morning, when I was finally able to speak to David again, I grinned and said, "I'm so glad I didn't leave for the rotisserie chicken."

Whatever happened in that room, it was the beginning—the inspiration to change my life. I desperately needed to do something different, but I didn't know what, how, or when. All I knew was that it had to shift. I couldn't live the rest of my life on the trajectory I was currently on—dissatisfied with every aspect of my existence.

Ideas ran through my mind: leave the job, shut down the business, hand over the apartment, move away from San Francisco. Maybe I'd change one aspect of my life. Maybe, if I was brave, I'd change all of them.

I wanted to be more connected to the creative and loving energy that I had experienced during the ceremony—to breathe freely. My life wasn't so bad. It was tolerable. On some days, it was even beautiful. But I felt stifled by it.

There was more for me—I was sure of it. A richer, fuller life. I simply had to claim it.

Chapter 6

Return to Reality

I wanted to remain in the palpable spiritual energy of the cere-mony, but instead I returned to the tangible physical world and the reality of my current life. Immediately after stepping out of the ceremonial home at the end of that weekend, I looked down at my phone and saw text messages from my boss. She was complain-ing about something related to an event that happened over the weekend.

I looked over at David. "Of course my boss sent me a bitchy text message."

I'd shared with him all of my frustrations about work on the drive over to the ceremony. His perspective was that I was not speaking my truth and standing in my authentic power in relation to her.

"Just ignore it, Christina," he said. "You don't have to respond to her now."

That was just one of the ways in which David and I differed: He took his time responding to people and situations. He tried to always express exactly what he wanted to say. My tendency, in contrast, was toward quick responses I sometimes regretted and then had to apologize for later.

The ceremony had inspired me, though, and made me realize that I was not aligned with the energy of my workplace. It had shown me a vision—or a feeling, rather—of how I wanted my life to be. Creative. Free.

I knew David was right. The one thing I could control was my response. So, for the time being, I chose not to respond.

When I returned home from the ceremony, my apartment, which was my shelter but also my mirror, was in disarray. Usually, whenever I went through a transformation, something in the apartment changed as well: I painted, redecorated rooms, and purchased new furniture. But this new shift was different. It was internal, not external.

I retreated to my bedroom. By this point, I had moved into the smallest and coziest room in the house—which was, unfortunately, also the noisiest, because it faced 24th Street and the bar directly across the street.

Lying on my bed, I texted people I had met at the ceremony. There were two women I'd connected with in particular, one who lived in Los Angeles and another who had just moved from Bali to the Bay Area. We were still unraveling the themes and messages from the ceremony. Each of us was questioning how to apply those deep spiritual lessons to our current external reality. One wanted to open a retreat center in Northern California, and another was considering moving. I was just starting to grasp the changes I wanted to see in my own life.

There was a peace budding inside me, but it didn't match the chaos of my external life. My housemate's moving boxes were lined up in the hallway. A few bags of extraneous items to be brought to Goodwill were piled out there as well.

For a year, I'd been living like a guest in my own house, attempting to avoid Lisa, who was moving out. We weren't talking to each other, which created a tense energy in the apartment. Meanwhile, Elle, a calm, sweet Canadian woman I'd found on Craigslist, was moving in. She was in her early thirties and had recently moved from Canada to be with her boyfriend. They'd broken up shortly after she arrived in San Francisco and she was slowly building a new life without him. After Lisa moved out, another friend, Chloe, would be the third housemate.

I knew that the change-up in housemates had more to do with my own desire for change than anything anyone else was doing. By asking Lisa to leave, I was avoiding a part of myself—the part of me that actually wanted to leave and wished those moving boxes were mine.

The apartment felt like golden handcuffs. Whenever friends came over, they often said, *Never leave. This apartment is too nice for a San Francisco rental. You'll never find a better deal.* Over the years, those words had lodged themselves into my subconscious. I'd come to believe everyone was right: I should never leave. I was attached to my apartment in a way that felt more like a relationship than anything else.

But a part of me understood that in order to find myself, I had to leave—and that it was finally time to take that leap.

For the entire year I lived with Lisa, I complained about living with her and her two cats. The living situation consumed me, even though some aspects of my life, like moving my floral design studio into a spare room in the apartment, had made my life easier. Finally, after hearing me complain almost daily at work for months on end, my boss, a no bullshit woman, finally said to me, "You have to ask her to move out. You can't live like this. You're never going to be happy." Little did she know that I felt the same way about my job as I did my apartment. I wanted to leave all of it behind.

I turned to Terra for advice, too. I often relied on her to help me speak my truth in situations. Terra pointed out that the world and people around us are sacred mirrors.

"What is it about this situation that frustrates you that is really a reflection of you?" she asked.

In part, I understood there was a fear there—a fear of becoming a woman in her forties who was still sharing an apartment with a roommate in Noe Valley. It frightened me that I was a few years away from that becoming my reality.

Even though it was my home, I didn't feel I had a voice there, didn't feel that I could express the challenges I was having living with Lisa. This was through no fault of her own; in fact, of all the housemates I'd had, she was probably one of the most willing to talk through the issues we had. There were words lodged deep within my throat that I realized had nothing to do with Lisa but were rather about something deeper, something related to home. And yet I continued to address my issues with passive aggression. I watched—judged, rather—from a distance.

The reality was that I didn't want cats in the apartment, and I resented her for the fact of their being there. I'd agreed to it when we'd discussed her moving in because she'd told me her boyfriend had recently died and I'd felt terrible—though in all the time we lived together, I never found out what happened to him. When she traveled to visit her family, I refused to take care of the cats—I didn't want to deal with them—so Lisa hired a cat sitter who stayed the night, which meant that instead of getting the house to myself when she was out of town, I stayed with a stranger.

It got to the point where I couldn't even stand to look at Lisa's furniture. Her bookshelves, tables, and dressers were all a deep brown, almost black, whereas my furniture and I was minimalist and light. When I walked by her room and saw her paisley bedspread, it reminded me of the couch we'd had when I was a kid in the seighties. All her belongings felt heavy to me, and for whatever reason, this triggered me.

The first Christmas after my mother passed, I became obsessed with decorations and with beautifying our home. I put up the six-foot tall fake tree we kept in storage, then bought an eight-foot tree with my own allowance to put up in the sunroom. It was as if I thought the more decorations, the more perfect our house looked, the less likely I'd be to focus on the unprocessed grief threatening to consume me.

Lisa's taste, so different from my own, threatened some sort of precarious balance inside of me. I came up with the solution to divide the apartment so that we each had our own separate living rooms and one shared room that would be our office.

Her living room was right off the kitchen, so every time people came over, they saw her space. "This is Lisa's living room," I would quickly explain, as if to say, *This isn't my furniture. That isn't my style.* I started to subtly offer suggestions for her space and even bought a console table, pillows, and a lamp to match her furniture, hoping to make it a little better. She seemed open to the suggestions and to incorporating whatever I purchased into the spaces that were designated as hers, but maybe she was biting her tongue.

Mostly, though, the problem was that Lisa was home all the time—which was something I couldn't complain about, because she had every right to be there as much as she wanted. She worked from home, so I understood why she was always there during the week, but she also never socialized on the weekends. I couldn't understand how someone could live so cooped up, and the effect of her stagnant energy permeated the apartment.

Terra's words resonated with me. My frustration with Lisa was a direct reflection of something that was agitating me about myself.

The Veil Between Two Worlds

She was making me see my own stagnant energy, and it was choking me. I was suffocating in our shared home—but it wasn't her fault.

I was beginning to understand that whatever is happening in our external reality is a reflection of our inner world. Even so, I couldn't seem to figure out how to shift my reality.

After my mother passed away, my father, Teresa, and I were like islands: we shared a vast ocean, but never touched above the water's surface—and whatever dim consciousness remained below stayed there. Although we had suffered the same loss, we were unable, and perhaps unwilling, to share each other's pain. We coexisted silently.

My mother's meticulous cleaning ritual hardly seemed necessary for the home that we now passed through but didn't seem to live in. Whenever it occurred to us, we performed basic cleaning—vacuuming, sweeping, spraying Windex on the kitchen counters and bathroom mirrors, just as my mother had done—but the pots and pans, once used daily, sat unused in the cupboards, collecting a fine, sticky dust. On occasion, my father cooked simple meals—packaged stir-fried noodles and *lap sung*, a Chinese sausage that my mother used to put in omelets. But my mother, who had been there every day when I came home from school, was no longer there, and neither were her warm, home-cooked meals. Now, when I came home, I often saw white plastic bags filled with Chinese takeout sitting on the kitchen counter

At home, my father shed his work clothes (one of the five or six button-ups and a pair of trousers that rotated through his wardrobe) and donned a worn, short-sleeved T-shirt and a softened pair of shorts. He rarely shopped for clothing, and even then only from necessity. If he found a shirt or pair of pants he liked that were reasonably priced, he would buy two or three and leave the extras sitting, still shrink-wrapped, on his closet shelf until he wore out the others.

He took no action to get rid of my mother's belongings. He gave her jewelry—her most valuable possession—to my aunts after the funeral, carefully distributing the rings, bracelets, and necklaces until there was nothing left in her jewelry box. The purple satin robe she had worn in the hospital still hung from a small hook against the back of the closet door. He never slept in my mother's queen-size bed, still covered in the navy blue, hunter green, and maroon paisley comforter that I would forever identify with the last phase of her life. Instead, he slept on the same twin bed he'd pushed up against the window—a tattered, light blue blanket, his only bedcover. He attached a reading lamp to an armoire that stood behind the mattress and rested his back against it while he read or watched television. If I passed by his room in the evening, I heard the faint gurgle of the television and saw the gentle flickering of its light through the crack at the bottom of the door.

My father's life in our house, during the months after my mother's death, can only be described as ghostlike. He moved slowly, carefully, as if he were a visitor in someone else's home. He would get home from work around five thirty and go straight to his room to take a nap. The house was so still I could hear the hardwood floors creak in the upstairs hallway, followed by the sound of my father's footsteps as he descended the stairs after waking up to get something to eat. I sat in the family room on the floor next to the coffee table, doing my homework or watching television. He never peeked his head into the family room to ask, *How are you doing, Tina?* The only sign of his presence, in fact, was the sound of his fork clinking against a Corningware plate as he ate dinner.

On Sunday evenings he always laid out, in crisp bills, an overly generous weekly allowance for me and my sister next to the telephone in the kitchen. I took the money, although it represented to me a kind of rent he had silently agreed to pay. I knew that giving us money was the only way my father knew to transmit his affection for us, but I would have preferred more direct communication. If he knew, in the morning, that he'd have to arrive home late after work, he didn't make a point to knock on our doors and relay this message to us. Rather, he left us a note in his doctor's scribble on a small Post-it, placing that, too, next to the kitchen phone: *Girls, I will be home at 7:30 tonight.*

Home felt empty without a mother, without a channel of communication to my father. I would continue to grapple with what we lost when we lost our mother—how much it changed the meaning, content, and contour of our lives—for years to come.

Those months and years after my mom's passing became foundational to how I viewed home. I began to compensate for the lack of feeling, warmth, and family center that had once been associated with home by focusing instead on the way it looked. I learned to arrange the contents of a home into something beautiful as an attempt to mask any absence that might lurk behind them. I latched on to the tangible, because it felt too overwhelming to open the portal to my intangible grief—to acknowledge the emptiness of my home, the loss of my mother, or the great chasm that had opened up between me and what was left of my family.

We were hungry ghosts haunting an empty house.

Every time I walked by Lisa's room, I saw the photo of her boyfriend who had passed away. I didn't know anything about him, and yet, for some reason, I felt his piercing stare. This got worse after one of my closest friends committed suicide by jumping off the Golden Gate Bridge during the time Lisa and I were living together.

This friend's death was the first big loss of someone dear to me since my mother had passed away. We'd gone to graduate school together—social psychology—and shared a way of viewing the world that involved deep processing, reflection, and probably overanalysis. We both spoke more about our feelings than we actually felt them; we both held trauma within us from childhood. Over time, I'd started to notice how his unexpressed trauma manifested itself through physical symptoms that he would fixate on. He often spoke about the discoloration of the skin on his face, although I never noticed it all. And in the month before he passed, he injured his foot and became obsessed with the pain, although doctors couldn't figure out what was wrong. It was clear to me that what he was identifying as physical pain was deep emotional trauma he had not healed.

About a month before Lisa moved out, one of her cats died. I watched from a distance as the cat withered away until it was almost skeletal. It was a sad thing to watch the dying cat, who was so frail, get picked on by the other cat, the larger one, who would still claw and bite it, preying on its weaknesses. Lisa seemed to believe the cat's health would improve; to me, it was obvious that it wouldn't. It wasn't my place to impose, but I wanted to scream, "I know nothing about cats, but I'm pretty sure yours is dying!"

I felt surrounded by grief—the grief of losing my friend to suicide, the grief of losing my mother, Lisa's grief over first her boyfriend and now her dying cat. It was a grief I wasn't ready to face, let alone heal, and yet living with Lisa forced me to look at it. For me, the apartment had become some sort of container, what felt like purgatory. There were so many lessons there for me to learn—about how to communicate effectively with people, for instance (something simple I'd never learned in my own home). But I didn't want to; I wanted to dispel the grief, to banish it from my apartment and from within myself.

What Destiny had said to me about the mother wound came back into my consciousness. Yes, I was aware of that loss, but—I was beginning to see—I was wrong about having healed from it. I hadn't. Not yet.

The Veil Between Two Worlds

And because that wound was still unhealed, what emerged while I lived with Lisa was that dark side of me—the harsh one, the mean one. Eileen, as David had coined her. I recognized her. I knew when she reared her head. She was my unprocessed grief, and until I tended to her, I would never tame her.

Chapter 7

Reverberations

Two months before my fortieth birthday, my sister called me from Indiana in the early morning, but my phone was on silent so I missed her call. I was sitting at a coffee shop in downtown San Francisco before work when I checked my phone and was surprised to see her number. We rarely talked, not even on holidays.

My father lived in Northern Virginia now—he'd moved there twenty years earlier, when I was living in Vietnam—and we never spoke on the phone either. He sent us online cards for the holidays and our birthdays, always sweet and heartfelt, often featuring cute animals. About once a month he would send a simple email to both of us: *Hi girls, How are you doing? The weather here is 70 degrees. Time to do yard work outside.* To which I would respond similarly—*It's warm here as well*—and my sister would write about her kids, Mya and Taylor, now teenagers. But we never called each other out of the blue simply to say hello or to catch up.

So when I saw a missed call from my sister, I knew immediately that something must be wrong.

The Veil Between Two Worlds

✦✦

The call I missed from Teresa that morning in San Francisco came on the heels of her having been sober for a few years, or so I thought. I called her back, and she didn't answer. I tried to text her and received only jumbled, incoherent messages that were not even words, just a mix of letters and numbers, in response. I waited anxiously throughout the day for her to return my call, trying not to fear the worst.

When I received a missed call from an unknown number in Indiana, I knew she was in trouble. Finally, her ex-husband called me to explain. She was in a medically induced coma. She'd called him that morning, panicking and unable to breathe. He'd immediately gone to pick her up and bring her to the emergency room. Three nurses had wrestled her to the ground in order to sedate and intubate her so she could breathe with a ventilator. Later, a nurse described her like a fish out of water. She didn't want to be contained. She didn't want to be intubated.

I called my father as soon as I heard the news.

"Who told you, Christina?" he asked defensively.

"TJ told me," I responded. "Are you going to see her?"

"Oh, I'm not sure."

My father was the one who'd given the go-ahead to put my sister in a medically induced coma earlier in the day. TJ and his mother were with my niece and nephew at my sister's home. TJ had called my father to ask for his permission to move ahead with the medical initiative, and I don't think anyone, especially my father, planned to inform me. Maybe he didn't want me to worry, but it infuriated me that I might have never known what was going on if Teresa herself hadn't tried to call me, and that my dad wasn't even sure whether he would travel to Indiana from Northern Virginia to see her.

A few days later, I arrived in Indianapolis. I called up one of my mother's friends, Mrs. Burns, to pick me up at the airport and drive me to Bloomington, unable to face the uncertainty of my sister's condition on my own.

Mrs. Burns was a nurse who had lived down the street from us when we first moved to Bedford, where I went to junior high and high school. She had loved my mother and had kept her hand-written recipes of beef and broccoli and stir fry chicken for decades before passing them along to me. She'd even kept a pot that my mother had brought over to her full of chicken soup once when she was sick. Her family had attended our church, and I'd been close with her eldest son. I needed a mother figure to hold me through this experience, to walk me through the hospital doors, because I knew that I was not really capable of doing it alone. Mrs. Burns was the perfect choice.

When we got there, my father was in the hospital lobby. Sunlight beamed through the skylights above. He looked forward stoically as he sat on a leather sofa a few feet away from the receptionist's desk. Staring straight ahead through the window, no phone, computer, or book to distract him, he wore a light blue T-shirt, dark gray dress pants, and brown loafers—the exact same outfit I remembered him wearing as his casual weekend attire when I was a child. While he had aged, and it had been two years since I'd last seen him, his demeanor was the same.

To my surprise, he greeted Mrs. Burns warmly. She'd worked in the same hospital where my father was a surgeon. She'd known about his quiet disposition from my mother, but had also mentioned to me in the past that he had a reputation of being incredibly caring, gentle, and soft-spoken with his patients. I couldn't imagine him being so attentive and available, since he wasn't that way with us.

The hospital was a familiar backdrop for our family, and fitting in some ways for us, emotionally distant as we were—a sterile, cold environment lit with fluorescent lights. Our young lives had revolved around the hospital, whether my father was on call or had to perform a surgery. I often waited for my father in his office. I'd take the school bus to his work, and then catch a ride back home with him. And later, when my mother was sick, we were in and out of hospitals for nine months for her chemotherapy and radiation treatments, plus the few times she was hospitalized during that period.

When she was in the last months of her life, we flew to the MD Anderson Cancer Center in Houston, Texas, to see whether they could help her. We carried her X-rays with us. The appointment lasted ten minutes. My mother walked out of the room quickly afterward; there was nothing they could do to help her. She had only a few months left to live.

My father led me and Mrs. Burns to my sister's room on the fourth floor of the intensive care unit. He navigated the hallways as if he'd been there for days. Although he walked only a few steps in front of me, I felt alone. Nurses wearing scrubs and hospital visitors passed us in the hallway, smiling and nodding. I grasped for their warmth as we turned into my sister's room.

There she was, lying on the hospital bed, looking so fragile, like a little bird with clipped wings. She was breathing with the support of a ventilator and deeply sedated, and I was instantaneously transported to being a helpless teenager watching my mother battle cancer. Twenty-five years had passed since my mother's death, but in that moment, it was as if nothing had changed for me emotionally in all that time.

It looked like tears were streaming down my sister's face. Her eyes were swollen shut. I asked the nurse whether a person could cry when they were in a coma. She said it was likely that her eyes were just watery. Her arms were bruised and poked from the IV. Tubes ran out of her nostrils—the lines connecting her to breath and to life. Through the slit in her hospital gown, I could see her swollen knee, the bad one she'd told me about when she'd complained about her aches and pains. It was obvious she had not been taking care of her body. When she'd mentioned her knee problems, I'd never imagined they were this bad. *Why didn't you love yourself more?* I wondered.

My father stood behind me outside of the room, not daring to move closer. "There, Christina," he said, pointing to the gloves and gown I would need to wear before entering the room.

I turned around and he was gone. I didn't want to go in, and certainly not alone. I wanted to leave like he had.

"You can talk to her," Mrs. Burns nudged me. "She can hear you." She touched my sister's face. "I love you, Teresa," she said gently.

But I couldn't find any words to say. I wanted to tell my sister that I loved her, that I was there for her. But I couldn't. She was in a coma, anyway, and I didn't believe Mrs. Burns that she could hear me. *Or what did it matter*, I rationalized, *if she couldn't understand me?*

Maybe that was why my father darted back to the lobby: There, one could be half-present and half-absent. Visible and invisible at once. It was easier that way.

Being with my sister in the hospital reminded me of when my mother had to have her colon removed because of a cancerous tumor.

My sister and I, both teenagers, stood on either side of her bed while Dr. Alexander, my father's colleague, held himself at distance, as if guarding the room's doorway.

"Your father isn't allowed to tell you this because it's against hospital policy," he began. "Your mother's cancer was not just in her colon. It has already spread to her lungs." He pulled an X-ray from a large manila envelope. "See this?" he asked quietly, pointing at the gauzy black-and-white images.

I saw nothing I could readily identify or comprehend.

With his free hand, he pointed at various areas—white speckles covering her ribs. "Those little white spots there. That's cancer. It's all over." His large eyes looked determined. He would finish what he'd begun here. "Your mother has six to eight months to live. I'm very sorry, girls."

The Veil Between Two Worlds

Dr. Alexander stood there a moment longer, looking at the floor. Then he inched his way out of the hospital room, clutching his clipboard tight to his chest.

My sister and I stared at him, at the blank doorway. We spoke not one word to each other. There was, at best, a glance shared between us.

My father walked in a few minutes after Dr. Alexander left.

I pictured the two men passing one another in the fluorescent-lit hallway minutes earlier. Dr. Alexander would have glanced at my father with a nod; perhaps he even uttered the words, "I told them." His face would have twitched, perhaps, conveying both helplessness and compassion, and most certainly relief that he wasn't in my father's shoes, making his way to a dying wife and two teenage daughters who'd just had their worlds turned upside down.

"So, girls—are you okay?" my father asked, without a hint of emotion, as he entered the room. The voice he was using was one I'd heard on only a few occasions—a voice that sounded strong and protective but also implied, *I know this is hard.*

I looked at my mother's face, the flatness in her small brown eyes. I grabbed hold of the only thought that seemed normal and real, to temporarily remove me from the situation: "I'm sorry, Mom, but can we still go to the movies tonight?"

This is how a teenage girl faces the incomprehensible.

"Yes, of course." She nodded. "Just go."

After that, we faced down her death. Since then, I'd held an understanding, lodged deep within me, that it's often easier to leave than it is to stay.

Now, looking down at my comatose sister, I wondered how I could gain the fortitude to stay—not simply in that hospital room with my sister, or in the room with my mother, but with all the emotions that lived within me.

Would I ever have the strength to sit with them without flinching—to express them fully?

Chapter 8

The Divine Feminine

The collective feminine energy created in the apartment during the months I lived with Elle and Chloe was similar to the energy I'd experienced at the end of my first ayahuasca ceremony. It was an energy I wanted to envelop myself in wherever I went.

Parts of me softened over these months. There was a gentleness in the environment that didn't feel forceful, but more like an allowing for whatever needed to unfold to transpire. I wondered if this was Grandmother Ayahuasca energy—the sentient spirit of Mother Nature. Whatever it was, I wanted to bask in it.

After all the years I'd lived there, I felt attuned to the spirit of my house, and I could sense that change was on the horizon. A shift was coming.

It was easier to balance the energy with two people than it was with just one. Elle, the Canadian, was low-key and easygoing. And because I'd known Chloe for years through mutual friends, there was a certain familiarity between us. While we weren't close, we shared a certain kinship; in some ways, she felt like a little sister to me. Her father had passed away around the time we first met—at a party at my apartment, which some mutual friends who were visiting from Amsterdam had invited her to. It just happened to be the first party Chloe had ever attended in the city.

We chatted that night, and I found her to be intelligent—she'd studied at a prestigious university as an undergrad, after which she'd attended graduate school abroad in the Netherlands—and open-minded, a trait I admired about her. While I didn't gravitate toward the same social life she did—late-night parties with her Burning Man crew—I appreciated her presence and perspective.

I thought Chloe would be a good roommate for me because she was cool and chill; I felt her relaxed nature would balance my sometimes wound-up personality, especially as it related to the home. More than anything, I was hoping she might love the place enough to care for it as I did. I had her in my sights as the person to take over the lease because I felt that the home needed someone like her—someone who was caring and community-oriented and not as controlling as me.

While I wanted to leave the apartment behind, I needed to leave it better than when I'd arrived. With Chloe and Elle, I could see a future for the place that I could live with.

When I first approached Chloe about moving in, she was open to the idea but also reluctant. She was aware of what had unfolded between me and Lisa, and there were moments of tension in our negotiations. I felt like it should be a no-brainer for her, because I was promising to hand over the place to her once I moved out permanently. But she had questions.

"I'm concerned about my stability in the home," she said. "I don't want to move in and then have to move out again if it doesn't work."

"I'm not that kind of person—to just kick people out," I said to her, though I of course recognized the inconsistency in that statement; I had just asked Lisa to leave. What I wanted to say to her was that I wouldn't do that to *her* because of our history and our friendship, but it was hard for me to find the right words.

Chloe's questions irked me; I felt like she was questioning my motives. She created a spreadsheet detailing the financial breakdown for the apartment and even did a calculation of the cost of each room based on square footage. I, meanwhile, didn't know how to make it clear to her that, while I imagined I must have seemed like a dictator in past situations, I actually wanted to create a peaceful, egalitarian home.

"What I want is to create a home life where people are free to come over and enjoy the space," I assured her. "I want to host women's circles and make it into a community-type space. We can even have a creative room. I want it to feel like a beautiful, shared home."

After about a week of thoughtful reflection, Chloe finally agreed to move in, and I felt relieved. I saw the vision of what she could create there, even better than what I was capable of.

This was the first time I'd ever had two female housemates—three women living together in the apartment. Our home felt lively and supportive. We kept the Christmas tree up well into February to maintain the festive spirit of the holidays. Chloe invited friends over and was often found cooking in the kitchen. I started using the living room as a space to host women's circles, inviting friends, who were often coaches, to lead discussions on various topics from intuition to manifestation. Every month, I also hosted one gathering where women came together to just talk and share the issues at the forefront of their minds. I also started an online Facebook group to reach a broader audience than women in the Bay Area. It turned out that there were many women who, like me, were yearning to be more connected to the collective feminine energy—the Divine Feminine—within each of us.

Chloe lived in a way that was noticeably different from my own. She spread out her notebooks, craft items, and yoga mat in common spaces. She owned a lot of knickknacks—memorabilia from her travels, art supplies, and little gifts from her friends—and she placed them not only in her room but also throughout the house. I began to see how contained my way of being was, and how in the past I had forced others to live that way too, expecting them to keep the common areas perfect. I'd never allowed former housemates to contribute to the decoration in the common rooms; I'd put all my personal belongings in my bedroom and expected others to do the same. With Chloe there, it became clear to me: I'd been asking people to live in a museum. For the first time, I could see how unfair it was that I'd been angry at Lisa for trying to make the place her home because I didn't like her choice of decorations.

I tried to allow Chloe to live more freely than I'd done with Lisa, but I had a hard time resisting the temptation to move her things around. She placed small succulents and other plants on the windowsill in the common living room and planted cuttings to grow more plants. All of this I found endearing, but also cluttered. I went around and replaced all the plastic she'd put under her plants with ceramic plates. And sometimes I would throw things away, like plastic knickknacks that looked like something nobody cared about. Once Chloe pointed out that one of her items was not trash: "I know it may look like it's junk, but it's special to me."

I appreciated Chloe's willingness to broach difficult topics. It was part of what she had learned about through her group training related to Nonviolent Communication and alternative forms of group therapy that didn't rely on traditional psychology and psychotherapy. We sometimes talked about the impact of growing up with Asian parents who had a tendency to avoid difficult conversations—and communication in general—and joked about creating another sort of unit in the apartment together, to help us reprogram some of the unhealthy patterns we'd picked up from our primary family unit.

Together, we planned to redo one of the common rooms by

painting it forest green, creating an earthy vibe with rattan baskets and plants scattered throughout the room. I shared images with her on Pinterest and brought home color swatches from paint stores for us to decide on a color.

Even though I was unsure of how long I would stay in the apartment, I also purchased a large, comfy white couch for the main living room.

Slowly, something started to shift within me. I wanted the home to look good, *and* I wanted people to feel comfortable there. I wanted to see something other than the minimalist vibe, and what I'd originally viewed as Chloe's more cluttered decorating aesthetic began to take root in our home without my feeling so agitated. The barrenness of my white walls grew tiresome to me.

As the one who was now suffocating, I had to admit to myself that I must have suffocated others as well.

One evening, Chloe and I decided to invite people over at the last minute. We texted friends and told them to stop by, and I made spaghetti Bolognese, a hearty dish that was easy to prepare for a group of people. Five or six people showed up, one carrying a bag full of laundry because she didn't have a washer and dryer at home.

There was an ease between us when people were over. Chloe had been to my parties over the years, and she recognized the effort I put into creating an experience. She was attentive and helpful.

"Should we use real plates?" she asked.

"Use the paper ones," I told her. "We don't do dishes on weekdays after parties."

She burst out laughing upon hearing this—yet another house rule she had only just discovered.

"I know you don't want to be a house mom," she said, "but can you be the cool house mom who drinks and lets the teenagers have a sip of the alcohol?"

The Veil Between Two Worlds

At the end of the night, as we were cleaning up, she told me, "You know, you don't have to have kids to be maternal."

"I know," I said.

She was acknowledging in me something fundamental to my identity—a maternal aspect of my personality that wanted to care for a home and tend to others around me in a caring way—and I appreciated that. But I knew there was another side within me as well, someone I was just getting to know: an insecure child. Somehow, I had to temper her. I had to meet her again and help her heal. Then the maternal woman within me, not the angry perfectionist one, would have room to flourish.

That was how I wanted to leave the place I'd called home for so long—in good hands, yes, but also knowing I'd evolved into becoming a nurturing woman who wasn't resentful of the roles she took on. While I still didn't have tangible plans for where or when I would go, I knew I would be leaving soon. The anniversary of my mother's death was at the end of April; then I'd be turning forty in October. I had both milestones in my sights. This would be a year for change and for resolution of the internal wounds that had held me back from relating completely and living wholly. At least that was what I hoped.

I was so eager for change. I didn't know I was still a few years away from becoming that woman I envisioned in my mind, or that even though I considered my relationship with the apartment almost complete, I still had another round to go.

Chapter 9

Đám Giỗ

A t the end of April, six months before my fortieth birthday, I
honored the twenty-fifth anniversary of my mother's passing. In the Vietnamese tradition, death anniversaries are celebrated
by hosting a Đám Giỗ, which is not a sorrowful occasion but rather
a festive time for family members to reunite and celebrate the lives
of those who have passed. The Vietnamese honor their ancestors
because they believe their spirits might wander in this world, as
well as visit with their human families, and they should be taken
care of.

A Đám Giỗ is a two-day event usually celebrated once a year at
the house of an elder family member. During the celebration, which
can pay tribute to more than one family member, an altar is created
with food and other offerings. Once the food is set on a table, the
eldest family member will pray and invite the spirits home. Burning
incense signifies the beginning of the ceremony, the invitation to the
spirits. Once the incense has burned, the spirits leave the home, and
the family celebrates and shares food while speaking of the deceased
family members' lives. On the second day, the main ritual, more

guests arrive with gifts such as fruit, wine, and baskets with tea, nuts, and alcohol for the altar.

My family never hosted a Đám Giỗ for my mother; in fact, we barely even acknowledged her death. Even when my mother was alive, my parents never brought Vietnamese traditions into our family life. They never explained why, but like many important aspects of our family life, I believe my father simply might not have had the words to explain, or maybe he thought my sister and I wouldn't care.

Most years, my sister and I would acknowledge our mother on Facebook, mentioning her passing and posting one of the few pictures we had of her—but every year as I got older, this began to feel less and less sufficient. Then David returned from his grandparents' Đám Giỗ in Southern California, and he shared with me how meaningful it had been to participate in this ceremony, which his family had asked him, rather than his other cousins, to lead in Vietnamese. He suggested we have one for the twenty-fourth anniversary of my mother's passing in 2018.

The moment he said the words, I knew it was something I needed to do. It saddened me to think that it had taken twenty-four years to invite my mother back to this realm.

David and I relied on friends more steeped in Vietnamese traditions to guide us in preparing for the ceremony. My friend's Vietnamese mother happened to be in town from Orange County, and she came to celebrate with us. When she saw the altar, she pointed at the various people in the photos and asked, "Are all those people in the photos dead?" Some of them, including my mother's sisters, were still alive; when I told her this, she asked us to take them down right away. I had no idea that putting images of people who are alive on the altar would be bad luck for them. Another Vietnamese friend who grew up in San Jose, a city with one of the largest Vietnamese populations in the US, explained to us that each bowl we put on the altar could feed five spirits. "Don't you want your mother to bring her spiritual friends, too?" she asked me.

During the planning process, David casually mentioned, "You know, you never really speak about your mom. I know about your loss, but I don't know what it was like for you to watch your mom die. I don't even know what your relationship with her was like."

David's cousin had lost his mother to cancer as a teenager, so David had some context for what it might have been like for me to have lost my mom so young. He'd often commented about the similarities between our experiences, but he'd never said this aloud until now.

He was right. I didn't talk about my mother. For so much of her life, I'd focused on her death that I didn't even know how to describe what my relationship with her had been when she was living.

"I don't really think much about our actual relationship," I said honestly. "It was her death that shaped me, not her life."

For so long I had focused only on the loss of my mother—on her absence. Now, twenty-four years had passed, and I finally felt that my relationship with her was beginning to change.

I wanted my mother's twenty-fifth Đám Giỗ, coinciding with the year I turned forty, to be special, a notch above the year prior. I wasn't sure if this was for her, or for me. Regardless, similar to how I'd planned my floral events, with the utmost attention to detail, I had a laser-like focus on this ceremony as the day approached. It was the beginning of something bigger—not just an invitation for my mother to visit my home but also a spiritual opening. I could still feel that beautiful feminine spiritual energy that had encompassed the room like a bright light at the ayahuasca ceremony. It was leading me to create a deeper connection to my mother in the spiritual realm. I was reminded that my mother was always with me, and all I needed to do was extend an invitation to her.

The Veil Between Two Worlds

I titled the upcoming event "Evelyn's Đám Giỗ" and created a Paperless Post invite for my closest friends. I used a beautiful black-and-white photo of my young mother, taken in Cambodia in the late 1960s, as the main image. She wore a white blouse with dark paint-like splashes—something I would have worn myself. I wrote the invitation as if it were cohosted by my mother and myself. I asked guests to bring their own photos of deceased relatives to place on the altar, which would help us remember them and invite them to be with us.

I hired a local sound healer I'd met at a yoga class to play the didgeridoo—a wind instrument developed by Aboriginal peoples of northern Australia—as people walked in. I turned my white tulip table into an altar and adorned it with tiny bright orange mandarins, soft pink rose petals, and eucalyptus leaves. I burned incense and lit a handful of candles of various sizes from six-inch pillars to small tea lights. Chloe placed a photo of her father on the altar. One of my closest friends forgot the picture of her father who'd passed away when she was in college, so she found a picture on her phone and placed her phone on the altar. Another friend from Guatemala brought an old black-and-white image of her grandfather leaning up against a car.

We lit the incense on the altar, officially opening the ceremony. The living room was packed with people—sitting on the couch, on the floor, and on chairs along the outside of the room. Of the handful of events I'd hosted, this was the most crowded. David invited each guest to pray at the altar and to pay tribute to the ancestors we were honoring. As people prayed, the veil would be lifted, and the spirits could descend. I felt a potent energy in the living room—dense, as if the spirit of my mother and whichever spirits she'd brought with her had entered. The weight of it felt otherworldly.

I'd bought a bright yellow designer dress from a consignment store down the street, thinking about how much my mother had loved designer clothes, to wear for the occasion. I sat beneath the altar, almost hidden, behind David and Terra, as David started things off.

He began by offering an overview of the event for the guests who weren't familiar with the Vietnamese tradition. "We're inviting our deceased ancestors to join us for this celebration," he explained. "We're paying tribute to their lives and making sure that they have what they need to travel in other realms."

"This is like the movie *Coco*, but different," my friend's six-year-old interjected, eliciting laughs from nearly everyone.

"Yes, exactly," David responded. "Like *Coco* but different."

When it was my turn to speak, I was nervous. It wasn't a performance. I was simply speaking about my mother's life. But I had never talked about my mother in front of a group of people. Up until the last moment, I was debating in my mind: Do I share my own story about my mother, do I talk about being motherless, or do I read the words my father read at her funeral?

Ultimately, I opted for his words—about being forced to leave Cambodia and then Vietnam, becoming a doctor, losing her son, working her way out of Vietnam to reunite with my father in the States, raising two children, and ultimately losing her battle with cancer. Then I sang a verse of "How Can I Help You Say Goodbye" by Patty Loveless—a song that was popular around the time of my mother's death.

That specific verse repeated in my mind in the months following her death. At the time, it felt like she was singing to me, and with every one of those words, I felt her presence.

When we ended the ceremony, the energy became celebratory, and people dispersed to the kitchen. One friend started pouring champagne, and everyone grabbed plates of Vietnamese food that I had picked up from a restaurant in San Jose. I wondered if our deceased ancestors were happy for us at that moment. Did they want us to live this way—honoring their memory but also celebrating life with the loved ones we still had? *Yes*, I decided.

That day felt like a celebration of my mother's life and her memory, and it was everything I'd imagined it to be—a bridge between the worlds, a joyful gathering with loved ones with the strength, wisdom, and guidance of our ancestors ever-present in the room and in our lives.

In the days after the Đám Giỗ, we kept the altar with the photos brought by friends in the living room. Each time Chloe and I prepared food, we placed small portions on the altar, almost as if we'd invited them to stay for the after-party. And indeed I felt their presence lingering.

It struck me that in the twenty-five years since my mother had passed, I had never once tried to connect with her in the spiritual realm. I understood now that the thin veil between the earthly and spiritual realms could drop away with a simple invitation. I wished I could call my father and sister to tell them about the Đám Giỗ, and I wished my father had taught us these Vietnamese traditions. I imagined, for both my sister and me, that having this otherworldly connection with my mother might have helped her.

So now I dared to ask her, "Mom, will you journey with me this year as I turn forty and enter this next stage of my life?"

Part Two:

THE MOTHER
WOUND

Chapter 9

Redefining Forty

D avid and I only had a rough plan for our road trip. We would start by spending the weekend of January 15, 2021, in Santa Barbara, where we'd attend the ceremony we'd signed up for, and then continue on to Ojai, where we would spend a night or two—I wanted to share with him the small town where I'd uncovered so many deeper lessons about my life. Beyond that, we discussed camping in Joshua Tree for a night, then passing through Arizona, potentially stopping to see his parents, before eventually landing in Santa Fe.

Even early on in our journey, I had a distinct notion that I might stay in Santa Fe for at least a few months afterward. David, however, was just along for the adventure. He didn't have a specific plan, which reminded me of where I'd been a year earlier, the first time I left San Francisco. Selfishly, I hoped that he might also want to stay in Santa Fe; I had only a few contacts there, and I felt being there with him would be a lot easier than doing it alone.

So much had happened in one year: I had lived in Ojai and then Santa Barbara; I had moved back to San Francisco for six months;

and now I was leaving once again. I hoped this time my move would be permanent.

When I left San Francisco in the fall of 2019, David was in the middle of a two-year energy healing program in Marin County, and I was busy redefining my life on all levels, from my work life to my personal life. I had coined that whole period of my life "Redefining Forty," because I hadn't seen many examples of forty-year-olds in my own life who had just packed up their bags to try something different.

Admittedly, I also spent a lot of time and energy during that phase on dating and figuring out what I wanted in a relationship.

In Santa Barbara, I was infatuated with Ben. I was fully cognizant that I was using dating to try to fill a void within me, but still, I thought Ben was someone I could have a real relationship with. I was blind to the fact that I was much more interested in him than he was in me.

Once during this time, I reached out to David, wanting to talk, and he suggested that I pay him for a session; he felt that what I needed was more than what a friend could ask for. "This will create more balance in the relationship," he said.

I paid him once but didn't do it again. It hurt me that he'd asked me to pay him, and while I understood where he was coming from—I knew I often overshared with people—I also felt that I was willing to be that friend for him as well. I wanted him to be able to rely on me, confide in me, and ask me for my support, just as I did with him. I wanted our friendship to be balanced. I just wasn't sure how to get it to that place.

My time in Santa Barbara was lonely, although I wouldn't have admitted it at the time. I wanted to claim an independent and free life, and yet I was trying to date someone who was taking up the majority of my mental energy.

What I was feeling on the inside felt contradictory to what I was portraying on the outside, particularly as it related to a Facebook community I was nurturing, which by that point had reached around one thousand members. I used the group to unload my reflections on being single, forty, and free. I found connection through this online community—connection I was lacking off-line. While I wasn't far from the Bay Area and made it back about every six weeks or so during that nine-month stint away, the changes I'd been going through were challenging to face alone. Women from the Facebook group messaged me and mentioned how inspiring they found the group to be. It helped me see patterns and trends among the women in the group. So many of us were seeking change, inspiration, and transformation. As I was discussing these topics in the group, I was working through them myself. Later, though, I understood that real-life connections would have been more beneficial to me during that time. I appeared to be claiming some independent life, but really I was just wading through standing water, trying to find solid ground.

And now here I was, going back to a place that held all those memories for me. When we were ten minutes outside of Santa Barbara on our way down the coast, David reminded me that we needed to stop at the grocery store to pick up food for the ceremony.

"Can we go to Lazy Acres?" I asked excitedly.

"Sure, we can go anywhere you want," he responded.

The desire bubbled up within me to share all the details of my Santa Barbara life with David. I wanted to tell him about an impromptu camping experience with Ben, where we stopped at Lazy Acres before leaving. I wanted to talk to him about my studio and how difficult it had been to make friends here. I wanted to let David know that there was nobody else I would rather be with on this journey. I also wanted to say to him, but didn't dare, that I often felt we had misunderstandings about each other–ideas of one another that needed to be revisited and revised.

Instead, I said, "Do you remember Ben, the guy I moved here to be closer to?"

"I think I remember him." David shrugged. "You dated a lot of men at that time. It's hard to keep all of them straight."

"Yes, but I really liked Ben. Really fell for him, in a way."

While we had not dated for long, the relationship with Ben had helped me peel back a layer of my tough exterior. It had felt like a starting point to becoming more vulnerable with people.

David knew the struggles I faced in romantic relationships. He faced similar obstacles to intimacy with the men he dated. His tendency was to be aloof, the classic avoidant, while I was always the pursuer; if I felt distant from someone I was dating, I would run toward them. He'd once told me that my relationships with men were likely the portal to my healing, and I believed he was right. It was where I'd faced the most wounding.

Surprisingly, it wasn't the loss of my mother but the absence and distance of my father that had impacted me the most. It was less emotionally daunting to think about the parent I had lost than it was to face the one who was still living. I'd always known there was a direct correlation between my inability to communicate with my father, even about the mundane aspects of my life, and my terrible track record with dating. It wasn't something I was proud of.

And David was right: I *had* dated a lot of men. During my time in Ojai and Santa Barbara, I'd continued to use my dating app in the Bay Area as well, so I'd often had multiple chats going with men in both Northern and Southern California. I'd joked with a friend that my goal was to have a boyfriend in both places, but my deeper desire was to be in a stable relationship. I just had to overcome myself to get there.

I changed the subject and asked David about how he felt about the ceremony being hosted at Sam's family's house. Sam was his ex-boyfriend whom he'd met working in New York. David had introduced him to the plant medicine community, which he was now actively involved in, and they'd broken up only recently, after the pandemic started. This would be the first time in a few months that David would see him.

"Oh, we're fine," he responded. "We've had a good talk about everything. And we're in other groups together, so this one isn't a big deal."

As much as I wanted a more intimate relationship for myself, I wanted one for David, too. We were on parallel motorbikes, after all, so I knew that what I craved, he craved as well. I worried that maybe we'd both been working on our inner worlds for too long—that maybe we needed to strengthen our toolbox in terms of intimacy, sharing, and vulnerability, things that required relating to the world outside us.

I thought about something else I wanted to share with David before we embarked on the ceremony.

"Isn't it crazy how Terra and Saanvi used to know each other?" I asked him. "I mean, what are the chances that you find a spiritual mentor and I find one around the same time, and it turns out they were once close to each other?"

"It's sort of strange, but not really, given our long history," he responded.

"Well, I just hope that we never let anything get in the way of our friendship like that," I said. "Not like after the fire. I hope we've moved beyond that point."

"I think we have," he said. "I think our friendship has endured a lot."

I agreed, but I still felt we weren't always fully honest and vulnerable with one another. Or at least I wasn't with him.

Chapter 10

The Veil

We arrived early in Summerland, the coastal town about ten minutes south of Santa Barbara where the ceremony was taking place. I'd been to the house once before, when David and Sam were staying there. The setting was memorable—beautiful and peaceful, and only ten feet away from the beach—and the house was big, with at least five bedrooms and multiple bathrooms. It would be a perfect space for a ceremony. And I was looking forward to attending a ceremony hosted by David's community in Southern California, too.

David and I picked up Chinese apple pears and other items to contribute to the shared meal that would follow the ceremony. This would be my third ceremony with David. I didn't know how many he'd attended—maybe twenty or more—but by now I was familiar with the process and the warm welcomes that David received from this community he was fully embraced by. I was envious that he had found his spiritual tribe. With the exception of my spiritual connection with Terra, I hadn't really found my own container to practice within; in fact, I didn't understand the path I was on at all.

Saanvi greeted us when we walked in and directed us to a large family room with burnt orange walls. "You guys can sleep in here," she said. "Or on the floor of the landing upstairs, or on any of the floors in the bedrooms. Just check in with the people who are sleeping there."

I hadn't seen Saanvi since the last ayahuasca ceremony, where I'd felt she'd been a bit hard on me. She and David were close; she was his spiritual teacher and mentor, but I knew she also relied on him for his support. On the drive down, he'd told me that she'd questioned his going on this road trip and pressed him about when he was returning to the Bay Area, since he had responsibilities to the community. Eventually, she'd said it would be fine if he attended the ceremonies he'd miss on Zoom but had made it clear that it wasn't ideal.

I didn't like the hold that Saanvi had over David—and while I admired her spiritual insight and her commitment to what she was creating, most of the time I didn't feel that she liked me much. She had a direct, tough-love approach, and she had clear favorites in the community. She also intimidated me. In her presence, I felt that I was always in danger of not being precise or spiritually awakened enough.

When I mentioned this to David, he reminded me that this was just how she was, insisting, "She's just direct in that way."

As I looked around at the twelve people who'd shown up for the ceremony, I saw that I recognized most of them from the two prior ceremonies I'd attended in the Bay Area. A few I didn't know arrived from Los Angeles, bringing with them a creative force that felt different to me. I later learned that one of them was well-established producer and another a feminist writer who had written the script of a Netflix series.

I admired their commitment to their creative path, something I had failed to follow through on myself. I wondered what would have happened if I had committed to my creativity and my craft earlier in my life and career. What if I'd simply claimed what I really wanted to be–a writer? I understood from what Terra told me years earlier, when we'd first met, that claiming a creative life was intertwined with my spiritual growth.

Would this be the year I finally made that claim?

In the previous two ayahuasca ceremonies I'd attended, there had been distinct moments when I'd felt I was entering into a more spiritual realm, a moment when it felt that the veil between the worlds had been lifted. The light and the entire feeling of the world around me had shifted, and my surroundings had become hazy.

In this ceremony, I didn't feel that transition. I recalled what David had told me once–that sometimes Grandmother energy, the medicine herself, is working within us well before the ceremony, even if we don't feel it so strongly. I thought I might not be allowing myself to fully surrender to what was unfolding. At the same time, when Saanvi invited all of us who didn't feel the medicine to have more, I declined, as did everyone else.

The next day, during the integration ceremony, several in the group shared that their experiences had been lighter, gentler than they were used to. I was surprised to hear how much other people's experiences paralleled my own.

"The energy was gentle last night," Saanvi confirmed. "This was the first ceremony *ever* where nobody asked for more of the medicine."

I was always nervous before it was my turn to share at the integration circle. I didn't know what would come out of me, and I wanted whatever I said to flow from my spirit rather than be conjured up by my mind. I resonated with the people who spoke before me that day–one who spoke about the gentleness of mother's love and wanting to be a mother; another who spoke of her deep love for her daughter, and at the same time her desire to understand her true purpose in the world. The writer from L.A. spoke immediately before me and discussed openly and vulnerably her self-criticism and the wounds of losing her parents when she was young.

While she shared, I thought about something Terra often said to me about women: *Women are the carriers of life. Even if a woman doesn't have children, she still knows how to carry life, to bring forth life, through her creativity.*

It dawned on me that this was the essence of what was shown to me during the ceremony: the power of a woman's maternal love.

When I opened my mouth to share, I didn't monitor what I wanted to say, I just spoke. I was surprised by what came through me.

"Similar to others' experience, my evening was gentle," I said. "Soft. Warm. It felt like being blanketed by a warm down cover. And then, what I understood this to be was the feeling of maternal love. A feeling that I haven't experienced most of my life, since my mother passed away when I was a teenager." I smiled. "I see that I want to learn how to bring that maternal love forth in everything that I do. I want to embody that love. And I want to give that love to the best of my ability every single day. That love is unique. It is special."

I finished by paraphrasing Terra: "Women are carriers of life. We know how to give birth to life from the depths of our wounds."

The next evening, I was in the middle of organizing my spot near the sliding door when Saanvi approached me.

"Can we chat outside?" she asked. "You're not in trouble, by the way."

She had barely spoken to me the entire weekend, and even though she said I wasn't in trouble, I knew she was going to point out something I'd done wrong. Bracing myself, I followed her back to the patio, where two chairs were set up.

Earlier in the day, I'd sat in this same spot eating a late breakfast with David and Sam. Saanvi had joined us and asked, nodding at my food, "What's she eating? I want that."

Immediately, Sam had responded, "I'll go make something for you."

This was the power Saanvi had over the community. I'd seen it with David, too. Whatever Saanvi said was gospel. And yet I knew that even the wisest spiritual teachers were still human. Or maybe I just wasn't as infatuated with Saanvi as they were.

She was undoubtedly a strong woman. I knew she was also single and around my age. I wondered if she had the support she needed, or if she sometimes desired the tenderness of an intimate romantic relationship, as I did, and used her strength as armor to hide that yearning.

"First of all," she said as we sat down, "your integration was really beautiful, but it was very binary in terms of gender. You know there's a trans woman in there. There are people who are nonbinary who plan to have children. And your comment about women giving birth to life is offensive to all those who plan to raise children."

I wanted to explain to her that she'd misunderstood my comment. I hadn't meant that all people, regardless of how they identified on the gender spectrum, couldn't be loving and nurturing parents. I hadn't meant to imply that the only way to be a mother was to birth a child. I didn't believe that. But I did feel that women were carriers of life, something a cisgender man was physiologically incapable of.

I wanted to say all of this—but I bit my tongue for fear of repercussion, for fear of not sounding enlightened enough. I didn't feel I could speak my truth—and this certainly wasn't the first time I'd felt that way in this community.

"I should've corrected you yesterday, but I thought it wouldn't be the right time," Saanvi finished.

"I'm sorry," I responded. "I didn't mean to offend anyone."

"Just apologize in the next integration. Tell them you had a long conversation with Saanvi and you are still working through understanding the full spectrum of gender, and you're sorry if you offended people."

"I'll acknowledge it," I said to her, but in my heart I didn't want to. What I really wanted to do was ask her why she didn't like me.

The conversation with Saanvi threw me off. Her approach felt jarring. We had barely spoken the entire day and a half we'd been there, and now the first thing I'd heard from her was criticism. I couldn't help but feel disconnected—from her, and from the others, too—when I walked back inside, and that set the tone for the entire second ceremony.

It became clear to me that weekend that what I was seeking in a spiritual teacher was a tone that was more loving, like Terra's. Sharp criticisms were difficult for me to swallow. I was looking for what I imagined was an ideal maternal love—something I wondered if I'd ever experienced.

One thing I regretted about losing my mother so early was that I never got to hear her speak about her fears, her dreams, and her hopes for herself as a woman. It was easy to idealize her after she died, and to remember the woman who was so devoted to her family. However, I knew and later understood that there was so much more to my mother than her role as my mother.

My mother was deeply afraid of the ocean—I distinctly remember the fear in her eyes—unwilling to swim or even wade in knee-deep water on our summer vacations. Instead, she watched us from a distance, covered in Coppertone sunscreen and wearing oversize sunglasses as she sat under a large, multicolored umbrella. She didn't want to study English when she arrived in the States in 1976, a year after my father, even though she had a secret love for languages in her twenties and had once dreamed of becoming an interpreter for the United Nations. Only when she met an elderly couple at church whom she wanted to befriend did she begin to understand the limitations of her language skills. She never got her driver's license, and rather than conquer her fear of driving, she relinquished her freedom and relied on my father and her friends for rides. Unlike my father, she didn't have the desire to undertake additional medical training to become a doctor in the States, although she had practiced in Vietnam and even earned a staff position at the French Grall Hospital in Saigon.

Once, when we were visiting my father's side of the family in California, I encountered my mother's fear on a local bus. We were on our way to my uncle's house, and as we stood clinging to a pole, a tall man with a mustache leaned over and whispered something in her ear. He must have thought she was beautiful, or exotic. I didn't hear what he said to her, but she was so frightened that at the next stop, she yanked Teresa and me off the bus and screamed for us to run. She bolted down the street without even looking back.

I had never seen my mother take flight like that before; she reminded me of a frightened bird, fleeing at the sight of danger. My sister and I ran behind her, trying to match her pace, shouting after her to stop or at the very least slow down.

That was the first and only time I remember her leaving us behind. She never told us what the man said, but the fear in her eyes told us all we needed to know.

I never thought my mother was beautiful, although there was evidence that proved otherwise. There were the photos, hidden in a tattered album at the bottom of a cardboard box next to the Christmas ornaments in the basement, that depicted a much younger version of my mother—stylish, slim, with a trendy bobbed haircut set off by bold-printed headbands. She was enchanting, although the look on her face, as she stood next to her brothers and sisters in front of a two-story building that must have been their home in Cambodia, was rather stoic. I could not distinguish at the time the difference between the two tropical countries—Cambodia, where my mother was born and raised, and Vietnam, where my mother would eventually meet my father in medical school.

There were other images of my mother and her sisters posing playfully around what I later learned was Phnom Penh, where my mother was born and lived until she was in her early twenties. I glanced at these images as a child and later devoured them as an adult, unable to reconcile the pictures of the woman in the photos with the one who ruled my existence, both when she was alive and after she was gone.

As I was growing up, my father would sometimes offer hints of another life, and he encouraged me to ask my mother to play ping-pong because she had once been a champion in Cambodia. She would always refuse, deny my father's claims, saying she was embarrassed or didn't know how to play. He once told me she had opened a Chinese takeout restaurant in Connecticut a few years after their arrival from Vietnam. I had no recollection of this restaurant. My father claimed that it eventually closed because my mother gave too much food away to her regular customers. She was too nice to be a businesswoman, he explained.

I never believed that my mother had the wherewithal to start and manage a restaurant on her own, just as I could never entirely accept the fact that she had once been a doctor, like my father, in Vietnam.

Chapter 11

Sacred Mirrors

In the circle that day, when it was my turn to state my intention, I blurted out, "My intention is that I don't want there to be separation between my life and ceremony. I don't want to have to go to a ceremony to feel connected to my spirituality." As Saanvi had suggested, I also apologized to the group for what I had said earlier, but I didn't tell them what Saanvi had wanted me to say, which was that she was helping me work through my misconceptions about gender, because she wasn't. I didn't view her as a mentor or teacher and felt that she only spoke to me when she was pointing out something I did wrong.

The rest of the evening, I replayed the conversation with Saanvi in my head. For at least an hour, without anyone noticing it, I sat outside where Saanvi and I had just sat, listening to the crashing waves. I started to feel anxious about the ceremony ending and realized I was ready to leave. I didn't want to be there anymore.

I wondered why Saanvi and Terra had a falling-out; then I compared my leadership style to Saanvi's. I, too, embodied that tough-love approach. I could be harsh with people and often wasn't proud of myself for that.

I remembered what Terra had said about "sacred mirrors." I could imagine her asking me, "And how do you see yourself in Saanvi, darling?"

I recalled a woman who had been part of my women's group two years earlier. I'd met her at a meditation studio, and she lived in my neighborhood, so we sometimes met for coffee. We slowly became friends, but I never completely trusted her, even though she attended all the women's events I hosted at my place. I noticed that she often spoke in a gossipy way about women who attended the circles, and one time even complained that one of the facilitators didn't like her and didn't give her the space to talk—which, I knew from having been there, wasn't true. At my mother's Đám Giỗ, she'd told one of my closest friends to take her daughter—a little girl I loved deeply and whose presence, even when she was making noise, never bothered me—outside the room.

Around that time, I'd also connected with a surfer in Santa Cruz on a dating app. I started to get excited about the prospect of dating him, and shared something about him in one of our groups. A few days later she texted me saying we needed to talk; when we did, she told me, "I don't know how serious you are about this guy, but he also started messaging me, and I thought you should know." It was common enough for friends to connect with the same person online—and in retrospect, I'd come to the realization that she was just trying to share information with me—but I took it as her trying to dampen my happiness. My response was to ask her not to attend any more of the events at my apartment. I wasn't proud of myself for that reaction, and we never spoke again after that.

Sacred mirrors, I thought to myself, and it dawned on me: I felt rejected by the community because of Saanvi's criticism. I had also rejected others in my own community that I had created. I began to wonder what it meant to truly lead like a strong woman. It seemed to me that doing so required being honest and direct, while also caring and compassionate. I didn't know how to do that, however, and didn't see strong examples around me.

I didn't felt like I'd made any progress at this ceremony. If anything, I'd spent the whole time in my head, processing—which was what I did all the time.

That night I fell asleep wondering why I'd even agreed to attend in the first place.

The next morning, I was the first one awake. I jumped in the shower quickly, so I could get out of the house before anyone woke up, and then took a walk along the beach.

As I strolled, I reflected on the previous evening's realizations. I felt distant and removed from the group—eager to leave.

The only place I could think to go was my favorite coffee shop down the street, a place I'd frequented often when I lived in Santa Barbara. I'd get a coffee and a chocolate croissant—two small treats that comforted me. Since the ceremony was over, I didn't feel like following the restrictions of the diet, although it was recommended to do so for at least another week afterward to fully feel the impact of the ayahuasca.

Minutes later I was sitting in the parking lot, inhaling the croissant. After swallowing the last bite, I realized that the only person I wanted to speak with was Terra. I texted her and asked if she could talk. I was relieved when she said she was available.

"Well, darling, how was the ceremony?"

I recapped what had happened, and mostly reiterated how I felt misunderstood by Saanvi.

"What do you think this is really about, sweetheart?" she asked in her typical fashion, pushing for me to delve deeper into the experience, to find the truth.

"I don't know, maybe she's upset because David and I are on

this road trip," I said. "He mentioned that she wasn't happy that he was leaving."

"What do you feel in your heart, darling?" she asked.

"I feel excluded. I feel she chooses favorites. And I feel frustrated that I apologized for something that wasn't at all meant to be offensive. I felt she misunderstood," I continued. "I feel she has her own wounds as a woman, as a strong woman who is holding space for so many people. Maybe she's jealous of my relationship with David."

I told Terra about the breakfast experience, and how Sam jumped up to make her what I was having.

For the first time, I broached the topic of their break with one another. "What happened with you and Saanvi?" I asked tentatively. I wanted to hear the story. I wanted to understand her experience with Saanvi, because I thought it might shed light on mine.

She told me that their falling-out had to do with a man that Lumi—a mutual friend of theirs, a medicine woman from Peru—was involved with. Shortly after they broke up, Saanvi started dating him, which upset Lumi. She and Saanvi asked Terra to mediate, and Saanvi felt Terra took Lumi's side. In their last encounter, Saanvi blasted Terra for all the ways she had been unfair to her.

I could imagine myself reacting similarly. I saw aspects of myself in Saanvi, and yet what I longed for right now was more tenderness and warmth. I was seeking women who exuded those qualities because I wanted to emulate them; I felt that was how I would make the change I wanted to make in my own life.

After my call with Terra, I drove back to the house and found David, who was just waking up.

"I really want to go," I told him. "I don't feel welcome here."

He searched my eyes, then nodded. "Sure. Just let me get my things together."

Later, I would recognize that in this moment, my intention was already unfolding: I was removing the separation between life and ceremony. Everything that was coming up for me there would soon be revealed to me in my life, too.

What I was going through wasn't about Saanvi, or about feeling excluded from the community. It wasn't about the story I had created around the experience, either. It was about me and the ways I showed up—and failed—as a leader.

I didn't know then how the medicine was working with me, how present Grandmother Ayahuasca was in my life. When a woman speaks her truth, she will be a villain in someone else's storyline. To the woman who I asked to leave my own community, I was the villain. And in my eyes, at that moment, Saanvi was the villain.

David and I packed up the car, and Sam walked outside to say goodbye. I didn't even return to the house to say goodbye to the other participants; I imagined no one would notice anyway.

As soon as we drove off the property and toward Ojai, I started to feel better.

By that point in our friendship, David knew when to push and when to step back. The only thing he said in this case, a few miles into our drive, was, "You know this isn't about Saanvi, don't you?"

"I know," I responded.

That was the end of the conversation.

Chapter 12

Silence

We were leaving Santa Barbara for Ojai, as planned. On the forty-five-minute drive, I thought about when my sister was in a coma.

I shared a hotel room in Indiana with my father while we waited to hear whatever information the hospital would deliver to us about my sister. The doctors hadn't determined the underlying health causes. Her ex mentioned that she'd been having breathing problems, which led the doctors to conclude that she'd had a severe asthma attack, worsened due to her smoking.

After a few days, not knowing when she'd emerge from the coma, we decided to drive back to my father's place in Virginia and return to check on her in a few days.

The morning of our departure, after three nights in a hotel, I heard my father move quietly through the hotel room, leaving the blinds closed. With little light, he fumbled to find something in his suitcase, then he quietly tiptoed around my bed to the bathroom. He stepped softly, trying to avoid taking up too much space.

The three days had been long and passed mostly in silence. He hadn't expressed any emotion, and neither had I. The only time we'd spent in the room was to sleep in the side-by-side queen beds. He'd spent most of his time in the hospital lobby, sitting and staring out the window with his arms crossed, or taking a nap back at the hotel, or running some basic errands.

Now, lying awake in the darkness, I listened while he went to the bathroom and then crawled back into his bed and under the covers, waiting for me to wake up. I heard unfamiliar sounds, which at first confused me, until I realized I was listening to my father cry.

In my nearly forty years, I had never once heard my father cry. I wanted to comfort him, but I was so startled that I didn't know how. I wanted to say it would be okay, but I wasn't sure if that was true—and I also knew he wouldn't want me to bear witness to his unusual show of emotion.

Having grown up in Vietnam during the Vietnam War, my father was a child of war and a veteran of loss. I thought he was immune to the full expression of human emotion. He'd lost friends who'd served in the South Vietnamese army; he'd lost his first child, a son, to dengue fever about a year after war ended; he'd lost his country to communism; he'd lost my mother; he'd since suffered a painful divorce from his second wife. Now he faced another potential loss—of his daughter—and it seemed the dam had finally broken.

Once my confusion passed, I realized that my father's tears felt hopeful to me, like rain after a long drought. If such a quiet and emotionless person could access his own emotions, maybe I could learn to do it too. I knew I was like him; that was the very reason his distant disposition bothered me so much.

My sister always reminded me of my lack of emotions. I remembered how, just a few days after my mother passed away, my sister asked me why I didn't cry when our mother died. I didn't know why. And now I wondered why seeing my sister in a coma didn't bring forth any emotions within me, either. I believed that deeper emotions, like the wellspring of tears one should tap into after their mother dies, were locked within me, waiting for the right moment to be unleashed.

Despite my desire to be open and vulnerable and to express my true feelings, I was often a closed book, able to intellectualize but not to feel. Part of the challenge for me was that I frequently felt overwhelmed by my emotions and couldn't find the words to articulate everything I was feeling. Maybe my father was the same way.

David and I rode most of the way to Ojai in silence, and I only exhaled once we entered downtown. Ojai, a small town with a population of 7,500, is nestled in the Topatopa Mountains and gets its name from an indigenous word meaning "moon"; the bohemian enclave is often referred to as the "Valley of the Moon." I've also heard people call it "The Nest."

Although David and I had just begun our adventure together, I felt exhausted from the ceremony and the realizations that had started to unfold there. I wanted to be in a place that felt safe to me. While I'd only lived in Ojai for three months, it felt like a safe refuge.

I remembered the first time I'd visited; it had been the start of feeling a deeper call of the land. It felt like Mother Nature herself had outstretched her arms and welcomed me to her nest.

That first arrival, which led to my ending up in Ojai for the month of my fortieth birthday, felt serendipitous. It had been preceded by my sister's hospitalization, which had brought up so many memories and feelings—especially around my mother. Even more so because we'd lost her at age forty-six, and Teresa was forty-two. When I looked at my own life and my forties looming ahead of me, I started to wonder if the women in my family weren't long for this life.

This is when I spoke to an Akashic Record reader, a person trained to open the record of our souls. She told me that I was undergoing a *life review*, which was uncommon for a person my age and usually happened to someone when they passed away. She said I was reflecting on the life I'd lived until now, learning from the lessons, and making the necessary changes for my future.

I knew I wasn't content with the life I was currently living, but I never could have imagined then that it would be another two years before the realizations would fully unfold.

During that first trip to Ojai, I rented a studio cottage as a birthday gift to myself. I viewed it as a time to decompress, to go inward, and to find a way to return to myself.

The only problem was that I was scared of sleeping alone in an empty home. Apartments, and my apartment in San Francisco in particular, didn't frighten me. Perhaps it was because there was a gate at the front of my building that prevented anyone from breaking in, and my apartment was on the third floor, and that felt safer. But I feared the spirits I sometimes felt lingered in homes.

The day I arrived was an unusually warm October day. Bev, the owner of the cottage, greeted me and showed me around the property. She was in her mid-fifties and originally from Australia.

She showed me her ceramics studio, which was adjacent to the cottage. "Sometimes you might hear me working late, or smell the burning of the kiln," she said. "I hope it doesn't bother you. I'm getting the place ready for the Ojai studio tour next weekend, so I'll be busy working this week."

"That's fine with me," I said, relieved that she would be close by.

When I looked in the backyard, I noticed a lonely yet immensely grand oak tree with a wooden swing hanging from an extended branch. It reminded me of Shel Silverstein's *The Giving Tree*. It was a perfect metaphor for the person I felt I'd become—depleted from overgiving and overextending, lost in busy city life. When I looked at that tree, I considered that I had lost a deeper connection with myself, which I hoped to retrieve during my time in Ojai.

"You'll hear roosters crowing in the morning," she said. "And the neighbors have two pigs, Cece and Bodi, so you might hear them on the other side of the fence, too."

After we were done with the tour, we paused for a moment at the door to the cottage.

"What brought you to Ojai?" she asked.

"I don't know." I shrugged. "A change. I was tired of city life. I'm turning forty. I wanted to give myself some peace as a gift."

"How long do you think you'll stay?"

"I'm not sure."

"You know, they call Ojai 'the nest' for a reason. A lot of people come here to nest. They also say it's one of those energy vortices, so you'll either be welcome here or it'll spit you back out if you're not meant to stay. You can ask the land if you want to stay longer. You can pray to it, and then you'll know."

The fact that she suggested I might pray to the land both stunned and delighted me. I was here, at least semiconsciously, because I knew I needed to reconnect to the land. I just didn't understand what that meant. I had no idea what my time in Ojai would uncover for me. All I knew was that it felt right at that moment.

Bev opened the cottage door to show me the inside.

"It's perfect," I exclaimed. It wasn't too big, and it wasn't too small either. Just one open space with a dining area, a queen-size bed nestled into the corner, and a small seating area. The place was vibrant: Multicolored tiles lined the wall of the kitchen. Brightly colored abstracts hung on the walls.

"My ex-husband is a painter," she explained. "Those are some of his paintings on the wall."

She told me a bit of her story—that she'd moved here from Australia with her ex, who then started having an affair with another woman in their spiritual community. "We moved out to Ojai, separated, and then I kept this land and built this home," she shared.

"I'm sorry," I said.

"It's okay. That was a long time ago. And life happens."

She reached to grab some pamphlets on the wooden desk by the door. "And I don't want to forget to give you these. I left some brochures of places to eat around town, and in the evenings you should watch the sunset. Here in Ojai, we call it the Pink Moment—when the sky takes on a soft, pinkish glow over the mountains. You can see it from the backyard."

That first evening, I made sure to watch the sunset. I felt peaceful, free of the distractions and demands of the life I had created and temporarily left behind in San Francisco. I felt wrapped in the warmth of the sunset's glow. I felt sure that Ojai would help me find something—maybe a tenderness within me, a place I had not yet discovered.

I'd only realize in retrospect that I was naive to think that one month of solitude would guide me back to myself. The journey was just beginning.

)C

Chapter 13

Soul Contracts

The Akashic Record reader who told me I was experiencing a *life review* also said that my sister had been negotiating a soul contract when she was in her coma. She explained to me that each soul carries wounds from its past lives, and comes to the physical plane to resolve those wounds and fulfill its purpose. As humans, we sometimes make decisions that are not aligned with our soul contracts, and this was what was happening with my sister. She'd been hurting her physical body for so long, and she wasn't advancing on her soul's path. She would have a choice: Did she want to end the current contract and move to another realm, or renew under different conditions? If she renewed, she would have to take care of her physical body and work toward fulfilling her soul's mission.

I wished that I could explain all of this to my sister when she was in her coma, but I knew that even if I could speak to her, the spiritual message wouldn't resonate with her. Still, I hoped that she'd emerge from the coma with a new lease on life—open to change and possibility rather than weighed down by daily life, work, and family responsibilities. I imagined inviting her to ceremonies or communities like Terra's, where she could receive support from other women. I allowed myself to fantasize about her being on a spiritual path, of us healing our familial wounds together, even though my sister had never expressed any interest in a spiritual practice in the past. I wanted her to fulfill her soul's purpose and to view her body as a temple that should be nurtured.

Mostly, though, I longed for a sister, and envisioned her coming out on the other side of this as a person who would be better to herself. I envisioned our family being there for one another in a way I thought family should be.

While we were in Virginia, waiting for my sister to emerge from the coma, my father, his long-term partner, and I drove to the National Shrine Grotto at Mount St. Mary's University in Maryland, a mountainside shrine featuring one of the oldest American replicas of the Lourdes Grotto in France, to pray for my sister. I drove, and my father gave directions from the backseat.

The fifteen-minute drive ended up taking forty, in part due to the pouring rain. When we arrived at the gates of the grotto, a parking lot attendant told us it had been closed for twenty minutes.

My father shrugged and said, "Oh well, next time."

I was frustrated that we hadn't checked the hours of operation before we left.

As I drove back onto the highway, my father told me to pull over at a restaurant adjacent to a gas station.

"Are you sure you want to go here?" I asked. The restaurant didn't seem like one my father would enjoy.

"Yes, let's go here—I've been here before," he assured me.

From wall to ceiling, the Irish-themed restaurant was decorated in shades of green ranging from deep forest to shamrock. There were good luck posters hanging on every wall and angel figurines lining the shelves. There wasn't an inch of wall space left unadorned. A singer and guitarist stood by a fireplace, playing music.

The decor reminded me of my sister, who got married on St. Patrick's Day, although I'd never asked if there was any particular reason she chose to marry on that day.

Being the only Asians among the fifty or so people dining in the packed restaurant made me uncomfortable—I was used to the diversity of the Bay Area—though it struck me, sitting there, that this was what my father and sister were accustomed to.

Surprisingly, my father appeared rather amused by the restaurant. As he looked around at the over-the-top decor and knickknacks, he smiled to himself.

It was only when I looked at the menu and saw the Maryland crab that the whole thing made sense. My father was a connoisseur of good seafood.

While we waited for the food, I looked down at my phone and noticed a missed call from Indiana. Knowing it must be from the hospital, I returned the call.

One of the nurses picked up. "Your sister is awake and she wants to talk to you."

A second later my sister was on the phone. "Christina," she said to me. "Christina, where are you? I need you. I just woke up. I was in a coma."

Her voice was slow, steady, and soft. A pure innocence came through the phone that I hadn't witnessed in Teresa for so long. I felt like I was speaking to the essence of my sister, the one I'd only ever seen glimpses of, in childhood. I wasn't talking to the sister in crisis. I wondered where she'd been my entire life.

Through all her crises in the past decade, even the time she felt suicidal, she'd never said, "I need you." None of us had ever said that to each other, actually. Maybe we would have been closer if we could only have admitted to that simple fact.

"I know," I told her. "I'm with dad, but we're in Virginia. We'll drive back as soon as we can. Just wait for us."

After I got off the phone, my father's partner, Thảo, said, "You should go back to Indiana immediately."

I knew she was right, but for some reason there was a reluctance within me to go back immediately. It wasn't because I didn't care. It was simply that I wasn't prepared to return.

After dinner, as we pulled out of the Irish restaurant, the clouds parted. The heavy rain stopped and a rainbow appeared. I believed it was a sign from my mother, reminding me that we were not alone.

It took us two days to get back to the hospital—through the same sliding doors, past the same receptionist's desk, taking the familiar hard left to the elevator and the elevator up to the fourth-floor ICU unit. I followed my father, trailing a few steps behind him. We entered the ICU unit and walked to my sister's room only to find it empty.

Seeing our confusion, one of the nurses grabbed our attention. "Teresa moved down the hall. I've never seen someone so ready to leave after being in a coma."

I expected and hoped to meet another version of my sister. At the very least I wanted to encounter the person who'd called me on the phone at the Irish restaurant.

We found her sitting up in bed, partially eaten hospital food on the cold metal table next to her. She seemed alert. She was a far cry from the person I'd seen days before, eyes swollen shut and attached to a machine to help her breathe.

Josh, my sister's closest friend from high school, and his wife, Sheila, were there. He'd been a loyal friend through the ups and downs, but I knew they rarely saw each other, even though they lived in the same town.

Teresa didn't have many friends. Mostly she socialized with the men she dated, and previously her ex-husband.

When we approached, Josh was telling Teresa how his mother had died in the first room that Teresa had been in, and that when he found out that was her room, he'd feared she would die too.

"I'm so glad you're still alive, Teresa," he said, tears streaming down his face.

Watching him, I wished that I could access such tender emotion. *That's how someone should respond after seeing a loved one emerge from a coma*, I thought.

Josh and Sheila left to give us time alone with Teresa.

We hadn't arrived with flowers or balloons. We didn't embrace her when we saw her. We didn't even tell her how happy we were that she was alive and well. Instead, we stood there, frozen like statues, seeming unable to even extend a loving arm around her shoulder. Neither of us even touched her. I imagined if my mother had been there, she would have doted on her and warmly embraced her.

"So, how are you, Teresa?" my father asked.

"I'm ready to go," she said. "The food here is terrible. Can you believe I was in a coma?"

As soon as she spoke, I realized nothing had changed about my sister. She remained single-mindedly focused on problems. That was one of the distinguishing factors between us: I saw possibilities, while my sister saw problems.

"Here, this is for you," my father said as he placed a plastic bag with six Vietnamese sandwiches on the table for her.

"You can have one now, one later, and save the rest for the kids," he instructed.

"Jennifer Sanders came by," my sister said, looking at me and ignoring the sandwiches. "She's a nurse here. She asked about you."

Jennifer was a childhood friend of mine I'd attended Catholic school with for one year and who'd often traveled with us on summer vacations. This was yet another person my sister could reach out to and befriend. I was already creating a list of people in my mind who could support her emotionally. Anyone but me.

"A lot of people have messaged asking how you're doing," I said. "You should respond to Aunt Aline. She's been worried about you."

Instead of acting like a sister, nurturing Teresa, I tried to push her to engage with other people. I longed for her to find a way to connect with others that was healthy and not centered on drugs, but she wasn't the type to reach out to people. In many ways, my sister and I were alike. We both shared this protective layer. As much as I was saying these things to her, I was also talking to myself.

"People care about you," I said.

"I know," she responded. "I'm messaging with Matthew now."

Matthew was her most recent ex, who had also been her first boyfriend when we'd moved to Indiana. He'd recently been released from prison, and while she considered him a childhood sweetheart, he didn't seem like the best person for her to date.

I didn't want to tell her that Matthew had reached out to me via Facebook the first day she was in a coma and, instead of being concerned about her, had listed his grievances toward her: he'd paid for my niece's soccer equipment, he'd recently bought Teresaan air conditioner, he'd tried to help her get her life in order. A few days later, he'd reached out to me again to tell me he wanted the air conditioner back, and the money she owed him. He clearly expected me or my father to pay him back. I didn't respond.

There was so much love and support available to her, but Teresa was fixated on messaging Matthew. I knew my mother's family would support her if she just asked, but I couldn't imagine Teresa reaching out to them. I knew I probably wouldn't either, if I found myself in a personal crisis.

My father stood at Teresa's bedside for a few more minutes before saying, "All right, Teresa, I'm going downstairs."

Anger boiled within me toward my father. *This is the moment you stay and don't leave. This is the moment she needs you. She needs us. Just five more minutes or ten more minutes. Just pull up a chair and sit in this room with her, with us. Why is that so hard?* I wondered.

My next thought was: *If you are allowed to leave, why can't I?*

My sister sensed my discomfort. "You can leave too, if you want."

I thought about all the times my sister had felt abandoned by us. I'd left after high school and never returned to Indiana. My father had moved three hours away from her to another town in Indiana, and then he'd moved to Virginia. My sister and my mother's grave were the only parts of our family left in Indiana. Every time she struggled with problem, we barely stayed with her. I think neither of us could sit through the pain of watching her self-destruct.

I flashed back to other times my father had left us, and how Liên, his second wife, had put distance between us even as she was the only means through which we could access him. In that moment, I felt my own sadness for him leaving, but also the wounds of my mother. I wondered if she'd ever asked him why he didn't return to Saigon to find her and his son when he was stationed in Phú Quốc, a Vietnamese island off the coast of Cambodia in the Gulf of Thailand, at the end of the war. Undoubtedly, it was safer for him to leave rather than live in Communist Vietnam, but other men stationed with my father had returned to find their families, so why hadn't he?

I remembered when I was five and we lived in Tennessee. My father left us at a butcher's shop twenty minutes away from home. My mother, my sister, and I were standing in a walk-in freezer looking at the flesh of the dead cows hanging from the ceiling, and when we turned around, my father was gone. The owner of the store had to drive us home. I never knew why he left us there.

When my father's relationship with Liên ended, the breaking point was that he didn't stay with her at the hospital when she was sick. There were other problems beyond that incident, but in the moment when she needed my father to be there with her, he'd left. Maybe being a surgeon for so long had desensitized him to other people's pain. Maybe through his eyes, a hospital was a place where you momentarily step in to attend to someone's pain and then leave. But we were not his patients, we were his family, and it was his daughter who was there on the hospital bed.

And yes, I did want to leave. I didn't want to sit with the emotions.

"I'm going to get coffee. Do you want anything?" I asked.

"Yes, get me a latte," Teresa said.

At that moment, I saw it so clearly: I was like my father. I couldn't stay with pain or discomfort. Maybe part of that was my father's wounding that I had inherited from him. A generational trauma passed down to me. Maybe leaving was associated with survival in his mind. He had to flee Vietnam; he had to leave everything behind to find freedom.

It didn't seem possible that at this stage in his life, my father was going to change. Leaving didn't have to equate to survival for *me*, however.

I wanted to become someone who could stay. But I wasn't there yet.

Chapter 14

Mother Figures

I met Siobhan in 2019 through another Bay Area transplant, Lei, with whom I had struck up a conversation at a yoga studio in Ojai on New Year's Day the previous year. Lei had moved to Ojai to live with her boyfriend, Dylan, who rented a room from Siobhan. When I ended things with Ben, I reached out to Lei and asked if I could come hang out with her and Dylan in Ojai.

The day I arrived, they showed me a secret spot near a creek in Ojai.

"It'll be healing for you," Lei told me, "and maybe later we can go to the hot springs. You could even stay the night if Siobhan is okay with it."

Based on the build-up around her, I was afraid to meet Siobhan. Lei and Dylan had told me she was returning from an ayahuasca ceremony and they weren't sure what mood she would be in. They also mentioned that sometimes she would invite people from the ceremony to stay over, so there might not be space for me. I didn't even have a change of clothes with me, but I wasn't ready to go back to my studio in Santa Barbara.

The Veil Between Two Worlds

When we got to her place, Siobhan was there. She was a petite, fit woman, probably only five feet tall but incredibly lean and muscular. Lei and Dylan told me that she had trained as a naturopathic doctor in Germany, where she was from originally. Somehow, she'd ended up in Ojai, where she'd had two kids and now ran a yoga studio and a healing center in town.

She embraced me with an effusive warmth that surprised me given what I had heard about her. "Welcome, Christina. They told me you live in Santa Barbara but were in Ojai before. Welcome back, baby. You're home now. And you're welcome to stay as long as you want."

I felt immediately welcome. Home was what I was looking for, was so desperately craving. It was odd to me that staying in a stranger's house felt more right to me in that moment than calling a friend in San Francisco, or even returning there for the weekend. I supposed I'd landed just where I needed to be.

One night at Siobhan's turned into a week. I returned to my studio in Santa Barbara to pick up clothes and quickly went back to Ojai. I could tell that I was back in a pattern of not wanting to sit still, this time in Santa Barbara. I was running away yet again, seeking emotional relief, no matter how temporary.

From the first evening I stayed with her, Siobhan claimed she was *working* on me, although I had no idea what that meant. She lit a fire in the living room, and at one point in the evening, I noticed she was sleeping on the floor. The next morning, she asked me if I felt better. When I told her I did, she said that she had prayed for me.

Whatever I was healing at that moment was not about the short relationship I had been in with Ben. It was something deeper—a yearning for a man to fill the hole I felt inside me. Ben fit the bill for what I wanted in a partner: he was handsome, intelligent, worldly, and active. I was embarrassed to admit that I had been seeking some sense of validation from him—that at least some part of me had believed that if he liked me, I'd be worthy. That's why, when it turned out he didn't like me as much as I liked him, it had hurt so much.

Siobhan recognized as well as I did that whatever I was going through wasn't about Ben. "You need to focus on yourself—heal yourself," she told me. "This isn't about someone else."

I felt the contradictions within me: I was supposedly on this solo adventure in Southern California, yet I could see I was seeking something external to help feel whole.

That week in Ojai was like a spiritual and physical boot camp. Siobhan did an assessment on me at her yoga studio. She asked me about my family history and my current life, putting together the details of my narrative. I witnessed her flashes of brilliance, which were often overshadowed by her instability. I watched her be so kind in one moment to her son, who was around ten, and then in the next moment, yell at him for not understanding something. I recalled something I had once written about my mother: how she showered me with love, and yet sometimes also towered over us in anger. Siobhan had similar qualities to my mother. Her decisiveness comforted me—especially since I was feeling so directionless.

She recommended that I clean up everything in my life, from my physical health to my diet. She made a list of the food I should eat during the week I stayed with her and suggested that I pick up a whole array of supplements from the local health food store.

I did as I was told.

One morning, Siobhan and I woke up early and went for a hike on the outskirts of town.

Immediately, she commented on my posture. "Stand up straight and breathe," she admonished me. "You're not even breathing when you walk. And you walk too slow,"

I didn't know what to say, so I just stood up straighter and walked faster to keep up with her.

"You need to walk fast for forty to forty-five minutes every day," she said. "Look at me. I'm forty-seven and I've had two kids. Look at my six-pack."

She lifted her shirt and I was indeed impressed.

"Don't eat sugar or anything artificial," she continued. "And you have to get hydrochloric acid and additional supplements."

I just let her speak. On the rare occasion that I made a comment, it was inevitably met with criticism.

"You need to be precise with your language," she chided me. "Don't use 'umms.' Think about what you're saying. Don't just say whatever is on your mind. Americans aren't precise when they use language. The way we speak is so important."

Siobhan still had a German accent, even though she'd lived in the States for more than twenty years. Sometimes, when she spoke to me, I felt as if she were some sort of drill sergeant, trying to get me into mental, physical, and emotional shape.

When we reached the summit, she instructed me to sit on a rock and meditate. All the information she offered felt overwhelming, and a lot of what she said I already knew, but I appreciated her direct approach. Most importantly, I understood and agreed with the essence of what she was saying with all of her advice: *Stop focusing on the external and turn your gaze to the internal.*

"Learn presence," she said now. "Breathe. Be in the moment."

With that, she found her own rock to meditate on and left me to my thoughts.

I glanced over at her and realized how much I preferred the calmer Siobhan to the drill sergeant. The movement back and forth between her various sides of self, or moods, was jarring.

"You're home now, baby," she said again on the way back to the car. "I'm so glad that you're here."

I appreciated her warmth, but by this point I'd realized that Siobhan's house wasn't a place I could call home. I had already lived in Ojai for three months, and I knew I wasn't going to stay any longer. Siobhan had decided to take me under her wing, but I was ready to leave the nest.

I thought about my friends and community in the Bay Area. In a short five and a half hours, I could return to my familiar comforts in San Francisco—to the people who knew me well and who I knew cared about me. Yet, here I was, trusting strangers to change my life. Meanwhile, I had put distance between myself and some of the people I cared about most.

I hadn't yet put the pieces together that I was looking for home. I wasn't sure why it couldn't be San Francisco, but so many ideas of my concept of home had shifted. That said, I felt torn the whole time I was with Siobhan. I was longing for something, shedding previous self-identities, but Ojai wasn't home.

When I decided to return to Santa Barbara, Siobhan suggested we discuss how we'd continue our "work" together. I knew she was about to ask me for compensation for the time we'd spent together. On some level, I was confused; she seemed to have chosen to help me out of kindness—taking me into her house, calling it my home. At the same time, however, I'd always understood that there would eventually need to be some sort of monetary exchange between us.

We met at a coffee shop in town. When we sat down, she asked me to pay her something, a small amount, for the work we'd already done.

"It's a lot of work, baby," she said. "All the advice I've been giving to you about nutrition, and even our walk together this morning, was part of the training."

I must have waited too long to respond, because she jumped in with an alternative. "We could also do a trade. I know you have a big network and seem to be savvy with business. You could help me with some administrative aspects of the business in exchange for our sessions."

A part of me felt deflated. Not that I expected Siobhan to offer anything for free, but what I wanted in this moment was a friend, not a trainer or a spiritual adviser.

At least I'd come to the realization that I needed to find a way to heal the wound within myself—a way to bring myself back home and not seek others to guide me there.

I handed Siobhan $150, all the cash that I had with me. "We can figure out the rest later, if we work together," I said—but I knew already that I had no intention of continuing my training with her.

I needed to find my own path to healing.

Chapter 15

Wounds

When I arrived in Ojai, I already knew it was time to address my relationship wounds, and the fact that I was using dating as a crutch. Before I even unpacked, however, I was already on a dating app, connecting with men in the area. I didn't attempt to make new friends or to build a community there. I focused on just two things: my spiritual development and dating. This might seem contradictory, but as David had pointed out, romantic relationships were very much my path to healing.

My first week there, I picked up one of the brochures Bev had left in the studio and noticed that there was an Asian noodle place up the street from the cottage. I missed the access to diverse food, particularly Asian restaurants, that the Bay Area had to offer, and something about the restaurant being up the street was comforting. I went to check it out.

This was the first time I met Nic, who was both the cook and the person taking orders. I went to the counter nand asked to see a menu. I sat down inside the near-empty restaurant, right as they were about to start getting ready to close, and tried to decide what I wanted to order.

I was attracted to Nic although he had a somewhat disheveled look, his curly hair pulled back in a short ponytail. He was wearing a black T-shirt for a heavy metal band I didn't recognize. He was warm and friendly with the guests, making jokes as they walked in. I assumed because of his tan and laid-back vibe that he was a surfer.

As I deliberated over what to order, he walked by my table. "Are you going to order something, or just stare at the menu?" he joked. He had a warm smile that felt welcoming and genuine.

"I'm just looking," I said shyly.

After I left, I messaged a friend in the Bay Area and told her that I'd met a cute guy at a restaurant. I wasn't yet sure why that encounter mattered, but somewhere deep down, I felt that it did.

Each time I returned to the restaurant, Nic and I flirted a little bit more.

One fall Saturday, which happened to be Ojai Day, an annual celebration where people gather to celebrate the city's history, I passed by the restaurant. It also happened to be a few days after I had ended things with Ben. I didn't even give myself time to process, I simply wanted to move on.

The front door was unlocked, but the lights were dim, and when Nic greeted me at the register, he told me they were closed because of Ojai Day.

"But I have a craving for fried rice," I told him. "I only have a small kitchenette in my place, so I don't cook a lot. And I miss the Asian food in the Bay Area."

He offered to make a dish for me and said that he had lived and worked in San Francisco at an Italian restaurant in North Beach before moving to Ojai.

We shared stories about our lives, and I felt a spark of connection.

✦✦

Nic was a catalyst for me, in a way. I realized early on that it wasn't a physical attraction that was drawing me to him. It was something else—something about him that I found comforting.

Our honeymoon period lasted only a week.

During that week, I visited him at the restaurant midafternoon every day. I sat at the counter and chatted with him about the random things that were going on in my mind while he worked in the kitchen, smoke blowing up in his face from the stove. We talked as he chopped vegetables and prepared for the early evening rush. He stood next to me and leaned in for kisses. We giggled when we looked at each other.

We went on an official date on Wednesday, the first day he had off that week, and I could sense his excitement. He asked me if I wanted to go out to dinner in Ventura or Santa Barbara, and excitedly listed all the restaurants we could potentially try. By this time, I understood that he knew food and loved eating out.

We decided to go to a small hole-in-the-wall dim sum restaurant in Ventura, then stop by Trader Joe's to load up on snacks, which he always seemed to need.

It was Christmastime, so the stores were decorated. I loved the holiday season, but I'd been feeling alone as Christmas approached, as I planned to stay in Ojai and had no one to celebrate with.

I held Nic's hand while we shopped, which made me feel like we were a couple and pushed away some of my loneliness in anticipation of the holidays. I noticed he seemed uncomfortable in the store, and grasped my hand tightly as we strolled the aisles.

On the way home from Ventura, he told me more about his family.

"I'm a loner," he said. "I don't trust people."

"I don't either," I said.

He smiled. "We're the same, you and I—the same kind of crazy."

He'd come from a broken family. His mother, an alcoholic, had passed away when he was in his early twenties. He had a brother whom he loved and seemed to be close to, but he lived in Colorado. Since his mother's death, Nic had been rather aimless.

"I don't really like being part of this world," he continued, "I've experienced it all. I've been in love. I've lost. I've given myself to my passion. There's nothing more that I really need from this physical experience."

We often talked about other dimensions, spirituality, and micro-dosing on mushrooms. Those were the conversations that inspired me. He spoke about other worlds, other ways of being, beyond what we experienced in front of us. He was different from most of the guys I'd dated. I could share everything that was on my mind—things that might have been too far out there for other people.

He had found his spiritual connection through the movement of the ocean and the connection of one's body to the water through surfing. He helped me understand that part of my journey was to find my own deeper spiritual connection. For him, it was surfing. What was it for me?

Nic and I hit the peak of our short romance quickly, and his delays and no-shows were disappointing to me. First, it was a phone call from the restaurantm saying, "They changed my schedule at work so I'm not going to be able to come over."

Another time he stopped by to tell me he had to drive to his dad's place, a few hours away, to help him with something.

"What kind of favor?" I asked.

"I don't want to tell you," he said.

Each time I felt a little more let down, but I didn't want to appear needy. "There's something about women in Ojai," he'd told me early on. "They become needy. You are not needy, but there's something . . . something similar between you and them."

For Nic, I started to realize, there was a fine line between unconventional thinking and not being able to function in the world. I started to think more about his behavior and lifestyle. His van was a mess—filled with cigarette butts, empty chip bags, and drink containers. While he had never allowed me to see his place, I imagined it was the same. He smoked incessantly. When he came over, I felt like a mother having to pick up after her son. He'd wake up in the middle of the night to smoke and snack, leaving crumbs everywhere in the kitchen. Whenever he left, I had to clean up the mess he'd left behind.

I already knew we didn't have a future together, but there was something about his patterns and inconsistency that fascinated me—something I knew I needed to make sense of. I tried to understand his behavior; I even did research to see if there was a term or label that would help me understand his behavior. His emotional distance was jarring for me, but I felt that if I just had a framework for understanding it, I wouldn't feel so unsettled.

One night he came over and was angry about a situation at work. The noodle place had closed down, so he'd started working at the owner's other restaurant downtown. None of the guys there liked him, or so he claimed. That evening, he had almost gotten in a fight with someone.

I began to see that Nic truly didn't trust anyone, just as he'd told me. We weren't the same after all: I found it hard to trust people, yes, but Nic's distrust of others was on another level.

When I realized this, I found a diagnosis that made sense to me: paranoia.

We decided to spend Christmas together. Nic casually mentioned that his surfing buddy had invited "us" to his place, saying, "I would never do things like that if I didn't have you in my life."

The Veil Between Two Worlds

He said he would prepare anything I wanted, so I planned out a Christmas menu: lamb chops with a pomegranate sauce, curried cauliflower, mashed potatoes, and a pear tart for dessert. I bought all the ingredients, excited about the meal.

It dawned on me on Christmas Eve, after I'd gone shopping, that the last thing Nic likely wanted to do after being in a restaurant all day was prepare a meal for me. I decided to surprise him by making all the food.

He showed up as he normally did, disheveled from work and smelling like kitchen grease. However, he was pleasantly surprised by the meal. "Nobody's ever done anything like that for me," he said. "Nobody's ever prepared such a nice meal for me."

We had planned to go to a movie that evening, but as we were getting ready, he couldn't find his keys. We searched the entire place, and his car, but couldn't find them. Then he realized he also couldn't find his driver's license, which he often casually threw on top of his sweatshirt when he walked in.

"I need those things," he said to me. "I have to get the registration for the van this week, and I need my license. This paperwork is hard for me to get. I have to find my license." He was insistent, agitated. "Have you seen my keys?" he asked again.

I kept insisting that I hadn't seen them. Then I checked in my purse—and his keys were there. I had no idea how they'd gotten there.

"Are you sure you don't have my license too?" he asked. "Ever since we've been hanging out, I can't find things."

"I must have accidentally put your keys in my bag," I said. "But I don't know about your driver's license."

"These things of the world aren't my thing," he said, shaking his head. "Do you know how long it took me to even get the license? And now I've lost it." His shoulders slumped. "I have to drive back to my place to look for it."

So off we went to his place, but by the time we got there, he didn't want to go to the movie anymore.

"I need to be alone," he said. "It's not you, but all of this stresses me out and I don't feel like being with anyone right now."

In that moment, a torrent of emotions rose up in me. I didn't know if it was from the ending with Ben, or from the disappointment of Nic canceling our plans, or something else entirely, but I started bawling like a little kid right there in front of Nic. The tears were not commensurate with the experience at hand, but I couldn't stop.

"It's not you," he said. "Nobody has ever been as nice to me as you. I told you that earlier. But I need to be alone. Just don't think it's you."

He gently held my hand and I heard the honesty and truth in his words, but my heart was crushed under the weight of my loneliness and despair. I believed that Nic not wanting to hang out was my responsibility, and that I'd ruined our Christmas Eve together.

The memory of my father leaving us on Christmas Eve, the first Christmas after my mother passed away, flashed in front of my eyes. Abandonment—that's what I was feeling deeply in my body. This experience was triggering the feelings of abandonment—from my mother passing, my father's emotional distance, my sister's problems. All of it was coming crashing to the surface. The dynamic of a person not being fully present was so familiar.

Emotional unavailability—that was the thread of familiarity that was suddenly so clear. It was present within my family; it was something I experienced with all the men I dated.

Nic never showed up again after that evening.

Chapter 16

To Bear Witness

Before David and I left San Francisco for our road trip, I'd called Siobhan, hoping we could crash with her for an evening or two when we passed through. I didn't know if David and she would get along, her house wasn't particularly comfortable, and I didn't feel close to her—yet I felt compelled to bring David there for some reason. I didn't understand it, but I had to trust my intuition.

Siobhan provoked something in me—and I was drawn to her for reasons I couldn't grasp. And like so many other experiences in my life, I desired for David to be a witness, to help me make sense of our dynamic, her role in my life.

Over a year earlier, when David was in his energy school program, we'd attended an event where a man spoke about synchronicities, the metaphysical world, and his perception of time. On the way back from the event, David had said something that triggered and upset me. I felt that he was not supporting me in what I was sharing.

Similar to what had happened with Nic, the strength of my emotional reaction in this moment was out of balance with what was happening. David was confused. He didn't understand why one comment had evoked so much emotion within me.

Suddenly, I started talking about another time, eight or nine years earlier, when I had just returned to San Francisco and didn't feel supported by our group of Vietnam friends. The emotions felt so raw and real to me it was as if we were back in that moment, even though so much time had passed since then.

I was so overwhelmed by my emotions, and David was so baffled by what was happening, that we didn't even realize where we were driving until we parked. and David looked out the window.

"Christina," he said. "Look where we are."

We were on Collingwood Street, parked immediately in front of the house we'd lived in after the apartment fire in Noe Valley.

"I think you're feeling the emotions from that time period," David said. "That's why you're so triggered and why we ended up here."

I shared with David how transported in time I'd felt as we were driving—how the emotions had felt like they were from another moment entirely. "I'm so glad you're here to see this, to see how we can go back to another moment in time and process those wounds," I told him.

"Me too," he responded.

I hoped our short time with Siobhan would prove similarly revealing.

David and I drove through downtown to the east side of Ojai, which was filled with beautiful orchards. We pulled up Siobhan's steep driveway and parked in front of the A-frame house set back in the woods.

When I'd called her from San Francisco, she'd told me that Lei and Dylan had broken up. Lei had moved back to the East Coast to be with her family. Dylan's mother and one of his dogs had both recently passed, too, so he was unavailable.

"If you stay here, you have to leave Dylan alone," she'd informed me. "He's mourning and doesn't want to speak to anyone, so don't contact him."

Now, as she greeted us at her door, she gave me a huge hug and said, "Welcome, home, honey bunny."

I pulled back from her embrace. I felt simultaneously drawn to her and repelled by her. I introduced her to David.

"Oh, *this* is David," she said. "When you mentioned you were bringing someone, I wasn't sure how I felt about it. But David. David seems okay."

When I'd spoken to Siobhan before our travels, she'd said she wanted to join the ceremony as well, and I'd had to explain that it was only open to people of color. Surprisingly, she hadn't reacted. She'd simply said she understood.

"So," she said now, "how was the ceremony?"

I let David respond. Soon, he and Siobhan were having an in-depth conversation about the ceremony, and about ayahuasca in general. I'd known this was a topic they would connect on.

"Who is your teacher? Where's she from?" Siobhan asked.

"She's half-Indian and spent some time studying with a spiritual teacher there."

"So she's half-Indian. Has she been to the Amazon to sit?" Siobhan asked. "I've sat with real teachers in the Amazon."

I checked out of the conversation immediately. I could hear them in the background, discussing the lineage of the medicine. The energy began to tense up as soon as David explained the parameters of the circle—that it was for people of color, or those who have been racialized white.

"You Americans," Siobhan said, "you think you know every-thing. I'm more nonwhite as a German than you are."

She turned around and stomped to the kitchen. David was sitting at the table with his back to her, so he couldn't see her, but I could see her clearly from where I was sitting. She made an angry face toward David, then stretched her arms out as if she were sending him bad energy. When she fumbled her way back to the living room a couple of minutes later, she accidentally kicked a brick loose from the fireplace's base as she leaned down to fix something, and she immediately erupted in anger. She stomped back to the kitchen.

David and I looked at each other.

"We should leave," I mouthed to David.

"Let's see, Christina," he said quietly. "I think it will be fine." He always brought more calm and patience to situations like these than I did.

I tried to change the subject with Siobhan once she emerged from the kitchen again. "Where's your son?" I asked.

"He's with his father, or he's here with me. Why?" she asked defensively. "Where do you think he is?"

Now *I* was the target of her anger. She was fierce, and more demeaning toward me than she had been toward David. In an instant, she seemed to have completely transformed.

"And you two," she continued on, "you think you know everything. Don't share anything I tell you with anyone in your network, Christina. I know you talk to a lot of women, and I don't want them to hear what I know. They are putting up 5G towers everywhere. It's not safe. Don't sleep next to your phone."

As soon as her rant ended, she was suddenly sweet again. "Let's go get some groceries and I'll make soup for both of you. You two need nourishing food after your ceremony. David, I love you." She looked at me, nodding at David. "He's a good one. He's like your guardian angel. He's your sibling. He takes care of you. You should take care of him, too."

She pointed at me and said, "And you, we need people like you. The light ones who bring people like us out of the depths of our healing."

The Veil Between Two Worlds

It was in moments like these when I appreciated Siobhan and I could see the wisdom of her spirituality, but the shifting of her moods left a lasting impact. I looked at David as if to subliminally convey, *We can go.*

He looked back and I could see that he was fine.

"While you guys go to the store, I'm going to pitch my tent outside if that's okay," David asked.

Siobhan nodded. "You're home now—both of you."

I slept on the futon that night. A year earlier, that same sofa had been my bed for the week I'd sought refuge at Siobhan's. It was comfortable, despite the occasional chaos of Siobhan's space. It was set up right against the window and across from a wood-burning stove. Layers of blankets added additional warmth.

Throughout the night, I heard Siobhan rumbling, and for the first time I had an irrational fear about my belongings—felt worried that she would go through my stuff, although she'd never done anything like that before. I recognized instantaneously that I didn't feel safe there anymore.

Early the next morning, around six thirty or seven, I heard David walk in to use the bathroom. I opened my eyes and in a hushed tone said, "Hey."

He walked over and kneeled at the edge of the futon.

"What do you think?" I asked him, referring to the situation.

"We can't stay here," he said. "We have to go."

"Okay," I said, sitting up. "Let's go before she wakes up."

"We don't have to leave so abruptly," he said. "We can do it slowly. We don't have to run from her."

"I don't know, I just want to go," I said.

"Okay. Let me get my things packed and I'll be ready in fifteen minutes."

"I'm going to go to the coffee shop," I said. "I'll come back to get you." I couldn't get out of there fast enough.

I walked out to my car feeling like we were part of some stealth operation, not wanting to wake Siobhan. As I loaded the car, I looked up and saw Dylan walking down the outside stairs.

"What are you doing here?" he asked with a surprised look on his face.

"I stayed the night here with my friend. Siobhan told me you were going through a lot and not to bother you. She said you weren't talking to anyone."

"That's not true," he said. "She's completely lost it."

"Yes, she seems a lot worse than before. What happened?"

"I don't know," he said. "She got back together with an ex who isn't good for her. She's thrown off."

I mentioned that David was in the back in a tent and that we were leaving. "Can I introduce you to him?" I'd wanted them to meet and had been disappointed when Siobhan had told me I should leave Dylan alone.

We walked over to David's tent and I could hear him fumbling with his belongings.

"David, David," I whispered, "Dylan's here. I want you to meet him."

He unzipped his tent, and Dylan and I peered in. They exchanged hellos, and I turned to go to my car, suddenly desperate to be off Siobhan's property. I felt almost panicked that Siobhan would wake up, see us leaving, feel offended, and scream at us.

I went to the Love Café, the coffee shop I had frequented the previous year. I searched for a hotel on my computer and booked one immediately for that night. By the time I returned to pick David up, he was ready to go. Siobhan was still upstairs when we left. I texted

The Veil Between Two Worlds

her and said another friend had offered us a place to stay, and we were leaving early so we wouldn't bother her.

Her response was short and sweet: *Have fun and take care of your-selves. It was wonderful to see you and to meet David.*

At that moment, I felt guilty that we'd left so abruptly, and yet the anxiety of staying made me feel like a child again. I felt stuck, like I wanted to leave but couldn't find my voice. It was as if the words were lodged in my throat.

On the way to the next hotel, David seemed bewildered. "In all the time we've known each other," he said, "I've never seen you respond to anyone like that. You're not someone who doesn't stand up for yourself. What is that all about?"

"I don't know," I said. "I don't know what it is." Then I blurted out, "My mom. I think that's how my mom loved me."

Similar to Nic, I never heard from Siobhan again. I was con-scious of the fact that I was running once more, that I often left things unresolved. And I knew David was right: We didn't need to leave so abruptly. We could have done everything slowly and said goodbye to Siobhan properly. It struck me, once again, how similar I was to my father, who had often left without warning and moved our family multiple times without ever explaining why we were kids. It dawned on me then: maybe on some level I was reliving his trauma from leaving behind Vietnam, the motherland. *And maybe in some instances, it's just easier to go because the pain of saying goodbye is simply too much to fathom,* I thought.

I saw more clearly than ever before how wounds and trauma could live through generations. It made me realize that when I was healing, it was not just for myself but also for my family.

I breathed a sigh of relief that David was there to bear witness to my healing journey. It was comforting to know that I wasn't doing it alone.

Chapter 17

The Shadow Side

Because so many years had passed since my mother's death, it was sometimes difficult to remember her imperfections. I was coming to the realization that I often viewed her as the ideal parent—the one who could have given me the love I needed if only she had survived. But I knew that was faulty thinking.

When I moved to San Francisco from Hanoi, in addition to wanting to develop closer ties with my family, I also started using writing as a way of healing. I primarily focused on my mother, her journey, and her history. I hired a writing coach who worked through every chapter with me, helping me improve my writing and storytelling.

At one session, he came into the coffee shop, put the chapter with his marks on it down in front of me, and said, "You know, your mom wasn't really normal. Her behavior was quite erratic when you were a child."

Nobody had ever read what I had written about my mother before then. His comment made me think, and I started to wonder if my mother had issues that I was unaware of. My sister had recently told me that she had been diagnosed with bipolar disorder; after doing some research, I'd learned that bipolar was often hereditary.

I emailed my father and asked if my mother had struggled at all with mental illness. He said she had, and told me that she'd been diagnosed as bipolar when they were in Vietnam. He said she'd been ashamed of it and hadn't wanted help.

After learning this information, I saw my mother differently. I didn't love her any less, but I began to understand how much she had suffered and endured in her lifetime, and I stopped idealizing her as I had before.

About a month before my road trip with David, I had started dating a guy in the Bay Area. All my relationships were short-lived at that time—likely because, on some level, I knew that I wouldn't be staying anywhere permanently. I didn't understand the nature of my connection with Trent, though; I wasn't physically attracted to him, and yet I felt drawn to spend time with him.

Trent rarely stayed the night with me and often asked questions that were benign but annoyed me. When I asked him why he asked so many questions, he told me that asking questions helped him get a handle on his environment.

A few weeks into dating him, I started to notice how he would sometimes fixate on certain issues. He also had a tendency to leave abruptly when we were hanging out, saying he was sick and had to go. Sometimes, when we texted one another, I felt that I was chatting with a different person—the tone and even the language didn't seem like him.

Once, after we went on a hike, he mentioned he wasn't feeling well and needed to stop at a grocery store. He insisted that I not come in with him. When we arrived back at my place, he wanted to go home, but I asked him to come inside with me.

We sat in my room together, and over a period of a few hours, I watched as different personalities came through Trent. He sat on the floor at the bottom of my bed. One moment he was Trent, and then all of sudden, he was rambling about another moment in time. He was free-associating, speaking about being in Haiti in the nineties with another soldier who was stationed with him, and how whoever that was didn't want to return to help a young woman who was being raped. Trent kept insisting they go back to get her. And then, just as fast as that scene had started, he launched into another, speaking to me as if I were his father who was in jail.

I was scared watching him go through whatever was going on.

Chloe was in the kitchen—I could hear her moving around—and yet I wasn't able to bring myself to leave my room.

It was a long time before I finally felt able to ask Trent to leave. As soon as he did, I called David and explained what had transpired that day. My focus, of course, was on Trent—but David was clear that it shouldn't be.

"This is something deeper," he said. "This isn't about Trent, Christina, this is big; I can feel it energetically. I think you need to process what this is really about."

As we spoke, I felt very similar to how I'd felt the night we'd ended up sitting in front of the house we'd lived in after the fire. Emotionally, I felt that I had been transported to another moment in time. Slowly, David helped me to realize that the dynamics I was experiencing with Trent mirrored how I'd felt with my mother as a child. This dynamic was another layer of healing that I needed to endure. Her mental illness had created a simultaneous closeness and a distance between us. I remembered her as being smothering and doting in one moment, then angry in another. My relationship with Trent brought that into my consciousness—the way in which my mother had loved me. I could now feel the pain of that.

Once again, a relationship with a man was serving as a portal to something deeper—another lesson brought into my awareness to help me heal.

The Veil Between Two Worlds

✦✦

Being back in Ojai with David made me understand that the first time I was there, something had been unfolding for me—I just hadn't been able to see it then. I couldn't explain it while I was living it. I had been healing, but I wouldn't have known to use those words at the time. I had viewed my time there as a simple stepping away from my normal life and routine so that I could see myself more clearly. Maybe that was a part of it. But really, it had been about healing and understanding on a sensory level that the only way to get to those early wounds was to feel them. Physically. In my body. To the point where tears would stream down my face with the gentlest movement in a yoga class.

I'd seen many therapists who'd asked me a variation on the same question: *Where do you feel emotions in your body?* But I could never pinpoint where I felt my emotions. I would respond that I didn't know. They would probe, *Is it in your chest area? What about your throat?* But I couldn't say.

In Ojai, I began to realize that I didn't feel emotions in my body at all. That's why I could never identify where those feelings lived. I could never locate them within myself because they were buried.

In the months leading up to this trip, I'd started seeing a new therapist. As soon as COVID hit, we'd pivoted to Zoom and started meeting every week on Friday at eight in the morning. I shared everything with him, from the status of my projects to the men I was dating. I disclosed more to him about the details of my life than I had to anyone. I never felt like he was trying to advise me or direct me. He asked questions to understand my perspective and to encourage me to explore a bit deeper. I thought he was brilliant and appreciated how he challenged me to probe beneath the anecdotes I shared. He recommended books, movies, and podcasts to me, and was always willing to listen to my take on spirituality, incorporating that perspective with more traditional psychology and healing.

In that fifty-minute container, I felt safe, maybe in a way that I'd never felt with anyone—certainly not with a man.

Whenever our sessions started, my speech was quick, and my thoughts were all over the place. I'd typically spend the first ten minutes venting about what was going on in my life.

He'd listen, and then at the right moment, he'd show me down by asking, "How are you feeling in your body, Christina?"

I didn't want to feel what was beneath the stories. Slowly, however, I became more open to exploring the question of why I didn't feel anything in my body.

"You have a lot of grief within you," he said. "A lot of grief."

"But my mother passed away so long ago. Why would I still have grief in my body?" I asked.

"We can carry grief from many experiences, not just death," he responded. "You faced a lot of loss with your father not being there for you, and also with your sister."

Every week in those sessions, I cried. These were tears that had started to emerge in Ojai and now felt like they were being unleashed. I could finally access a deeper reservoir of emotion. I was peeling away the layers of my wounds. I realized there was so much more beneath the stories I vented about—so many overlapping emotions and pain. I remembered what another therapist had once told me—that there was more beneath the anger and other primary emotions we typically focus on. Underneath my tears, I finally started to feel the pain.

"Let me ask you something," my therapist asked me one day. "Do you feel that you've ever truly been seen?"

"No," I responded immediately.

He told me what he'd experienced of me through our sessions—that I'd never felt my needs had been met emotionally in my family or, subsequently, in my relationships. "Your picker is a little off in terms of who you date," he said, "but mostly I believe you are always scanning to see if you're safe in a relationship or environment. And probably more times than not, you're erring on the side that you're not safe. But if you opened yourself up to people, you could start to trust them and feel safe with those who have the capacity to hold you."

"But what can I do to change this?" I asked.

"Well, first starting in this therapeutic relationship, we'll have interactions where you can feel seen and heard. You'll begin to be able to understand what that feels like."

"I don't want to be a lone wolf," I told him. "I'd prefer to learn to live with a pack."

"And you can do that," he responded. "It just takes some practice, patience, and understanding."

He'd accurately described me, but also my father. These parallels between us were becoming increasingly hard to ignore. I feared that later in life I might still be living this way: free and independent, but also lonely. I pictured how the two of us existed in his home when I was a teenager—barely interacting, sometimes not seeing each other for an entire day. We were both lone wolves, even though we were part of a pack. We were a family unit that didn't know it was a unit.

These weekly sessions helped me peel through the layers of grief and support me to access feelings rather than ideas I had about feelings. But while most of this progress was made in San Francisco, I came to realize that the process had started in Ojai.

Ojai, it turned out, was an energetic vortex for me. And now I was back in it.

Chapter 18

Grounding

D avid and I had only been away from the Bay Area for five days, and yet it felt like an eternity after our intense evening at Siobhan's. The thought of spending only one or two more nights in Ojai before hitting the road again exhausted me. I wanted to stay in one place for a week or two. I thought we both needed time to process all that had happened.

As I thought about this, the word *grounding* immediately came to my mind. Though now, with the energy of Ojai weighing on me the way it was, I didn't imagine we'd stay there, I did finally feel a sense of clarity around the place. I could see what lessons had been brought to my awareness in 2019. The purpose of my return there now with David was to allow him to be a witness to my healing and, as he always had been, a source of support to process what was happening. Now I was focused on the final destination: Santa Fe.

But before we left, I hoped to see Himari.

I was introduced to Himari through her best friend, Julia, a healer I met while working on a project. In our first conversation, Julia and I spoke for hours about life and healing. When I told her I was in Ojai, she said I had to meet her best friend, Himari, who was opening up a housewares store on the main street downtown. The two women had met in Santa Fe; their children had gone to school together there. Himari was on a trip to Japan, visiting with family and sourcing items for her store, but Julia promised to introduce us as soon as she returned.

While I didn't realize it at the time, I was seeking support, love, and guidance, particularly from a mother figure. I idealized Himari before I'd even met her. I'd imagined her to be a sophisticated woman, since she was in Japan shopping for the housewares store that she'd open soon.

Our first meeting was serendipitous. I was at a coffee shop when an elegant older woman approached me one morning out of the blue, asking, "Are you Christina?"

"Yes," I responded.

"I'm Himari, Julia's friend. We were messaging the other day."

I felt an instantaneous connection with her. She was warm and welcoming, and exuded a sense of calm.

"Let's take a selfie together and send it to Julia," she suggested.

Before meeting, I was already grateful that she was willing to take me under her wing. I hadn't realized until that moment that I needed to meet Himari. She made me think about my mother—made me wonder what type of relationship we'd have if she was still alive.

"You know, where you're staying isn't the safest neighborhood in town," she said that first evening.

"I didn't realize there were unsafe parts in Ojai," I told her. "I thought it was all safe."

"Well, by safe, I just mean that people are known to have a lot of parties over there," she explained. "Maybe some of them get out of hand. That's all. I know a property agent who might be able to help you, too."

She offered to help me look around at other neighborhoods in Ojai. I gratefully accepted.

The next day, when we reconnected, she told me, "Someone at the café said we resembled each other."

She said she was flattered, but I was ecstatic over the compliment. I found her to be elegant and graceful. She radiated a sense of peace that I'd eventually learn was not only a reflection of her soul but the result of the inner spiritual work she'd committed to.

She was easy to open up to, and I shared with her all the reflections I was having around turning forty and being single, childless, and motherless.

"I started having children when I was around your age," she said.

I was surprised to learn she was in her early sixties; she looked so young and radiant.

She drove me to the east side of town. She showed me her apartment and one of the spiritual centers in town, which also had daily rentals.

Spending time with her, I began to understand what it felt like to be mothered gently by someone, and what I had missed out on for twenty-five years of my life. I felt something, finally, in my chest, and I was able to identify it as sadness.

After David and I left Siobhan's, I texted Himari, asking if she was available. She responded that the store wasn't open because of COVID, and that she'd been turning inward during this time, not seeing others—partly because of the pandemic, but also in order to take some personal time. While it saddened me that we weren't able to touch base, I understood that we meet people when we need to. I hoped to see Himari again, but I also felt she'd already played the role she was meant to play for me: she'd been a catalyst for my journey to address the mother wound.

The Veil Between Two Worlds

With no one else to see in Ojai, my sights turned fully to Santa Fe.

My heart had actually been set on Santa Fe for a while. I'd visited a friend there in the fall of 2019, after my sister's health scare, and had immediately felt drawn to the place. Himari had raised her kids there. There was a similarity between Ojai and Santa Fe in that both places held a deep spiritual energy. When I once mentioned to Himari that I'd almost gone to Santa Fe instead of Ojai, she'd told me, "Santa Fe has a darker underbelly."

Since David was more methodical about his decision-making than I was, I had to be careful about how I approached anything like a longer-term plan. I started to search online for a place where we might stay. On our third morning in Ojai, while David went for a hike, I discovered a bed and breakfast that was taking weekly rentals at a reduced rate because of the pandemic.

Instead of waiting for an email response, I called and spoke to the owner-manager, Jess. She told me where the inn was located, just a little bit outside of town, and how she'd wound up in Santa Fe with her partner after both of them had spent most of their lives on the East Coast.

"We just ended up here," she told me. "I liked it, and my partner and I were looking for someplace to move, and we ended up here." She chuckled. "It just happens. People just move here. That's why it's called the Land of Enchantment—or Land of Entrapment, some say."

When David returned from his hike, I couldn't contain my excitement. "I think I found a place for us to stay in Santa Fe," I blurted out. "It's nice and affordable for a weekly rental. There's a small room with two beds. There's only a small kitchenette, but we can always just buy simple things, like soup and salads. And the manager is so nice. You have to talk to her. She shared with me all these tips about Santa Fe. I think this could work."

"Let's think about it a bit," he said. "Show me some pictures."

He was matter-of-fact and subdued—unmoved, even—which was the opposite of how I felt in that moment.

David hadn't expressed a clear desire to be anywhere in particular, but he knew Santa Fe had been my intended destination from the beginning. That didn't necessarily mean he planned to come with me, though.

"I think we should just take it," I pressed. "It's better to secure it so we don't have to worry about where we're staying anymore."

Even though we'd just begun our trip together, I was already sensing the distance growing between us, and noticing more and more the differences in how we moved through the world. I wanted to move quickly on to the next thing, while David was always deliberate. There was no right or wrong, just differences, but I worried about how we'd fare together over these next weeks and months if we stayed together.

I finally convinced David to call Jess. He, too, was moved by her warmth and openness. These were traits that neither of us was used to after having lived in cities for so long.

"Oh, my God, Jess is so nice," he said after he got off the phone with her. "Let's book this place."

I smiled. We had a plan.

The Christmas when I was in Ojai, my father mailed me a check to buy a plane ticket to visit him over the holidays. He sent it to my San Francisco address, however, so I never received it. I understood this was his way of asking me to visit him—by sending me money to buy a plane ticket—but I wished, as always, that he were a better communicator.

I visited my father once during the pandemic. Again, he initiated the trip, which made it clearer to me that he was getting older and needed company. Or, specifically, he wanted to see his daughters.

Although he was in his seventies, he still worked and, up until the pandemic, had still gone into an office a few times a week. I never asked him the reasons he didn't retire; I was pretty sure I knew why. He loved to keep his mind active and to be involved with projects. He also still helped my sister financially.

I imagined pandemic life for my father must not have been very different from his normal life. He was used to being alone—sitting in his four-bedroom, two-story home and tending to his yard on the weekends. I was also accustomed to my solitude, and in many ways I found it to be comforting and productive. But things had started to stir within me, and I couldn't help but wonder if my father had ever had a moment where he looked at his life and desired to be less isolated, more connected.

With the realizations I had in Ojai about myself and about my mother, I also began to look at my father differently. I understood how easy it was to misunderstand my father because of his silent nature; I was guilty of similar behavior myself, after all. I also began to understand, at a deeper level, that he had done the best he could in all of our relationships. He'd tended to an important side of the family structure—the creation of home, the provision of stability and resources. I could also see, after reexperiencing what it had been like as a child to relate to my mother, how challenging her mental illness must have been for him. I remembered hearing the fights and my mother claiming that the three of us would leave and live together—this despite the fact that she never worked and never even got her driver's license in the US.

When I was in my late twenties, I visited my mother's two sisters and my two cousins in Paris. They asked about my father and specifically about his divorce from Liên, my stepmother.

"See," my aunt Odette joked, "she couldn't stay with your dad either."

While I loved my aunts, this comment brought forth my allegiance to my father. Hurt on his behalf, I cried. I told them that even though my father was imperfect and quiet, he was a good man, and the ending of that relationship, just like the loss of my mother, had saddened him. He was human, even if he didn't allow others to see or understand his emotions.

At that time, I was living in Geneva, and after I returned home from Paris, I wrote my father and sister an email asking them why they never called, never asked questions, never seemed to care about my life.

I thought I was being honest, but really I was just being hurtful.

My father responded that he was always available if I wanted to write to him and share my thoughts with him; he would always respond. My sister said that I was the one who was leaving all the time and thought that I was better than them. That hurt, too. Hearing their perspective drove home for me the truth that relationships are indeed two-sided, and I had contributed to our lack of connection as a trio.

Since coming out of her coma, I'd noticed, my sister had been more interested in personal development, self-help books, and, to some extent, spirituality. She sometimes messaged me and asked questions; when she did, I directed her to coaches and authors who had helped me—but those exchanges never lasted long, and we remained distant from one another.

I wanted to tell Teresa how much work was required to really work on oneself, to truly touch one's wounds. I also wanted to tell her that I knew her wounds because they were mine as well. I knew she was a good mother, and that she mothered in a way that was doting and all-encompassing, much like our mother had. In spite of all her ups and downs, she remained committed to her children, and they had turned out to be good kids. But I knew she still missed that maternal love we'd lost when our mother passed away. This was the essence of what we both sought We were both numbing our pain, just in different ways.

Our journey, while externally it looked quite different, was internally the same: a quest to learn how to give and receive all the love, both maternal and paternal, we felt we lacked. This was the path to healing. But the road there was a long one.

I'd heard people say about both Ojai and Santa Fe that if you were not meant to be there, you'd be pushed out. I didn't like to think of it in that way, as if the land selected some people to stay and some to leave. I preferred to frame it this way: certain places have the right energetic frequency for a person to learn the lessons they need at that moment in time.

I'd only needed three months in Ojai. In the end I'd never prayed to the land, as Bev had suggested, about whether or not I should stay there, but I'd known it wasn't my forever place, and I'd understood when my time there was done.

As David and I packed up our bags for the next leg of our road trip, I reflected on those three months I'd spent in Ojai. Three months; three different homes rented to me by single women in their sixties. I thought about each home I'd stayed in, and how on some level each one had been a sacred mirror for me. I'd seen a bit of myself in each of the women I'd rented from and in each of the homes I'd stayed in. All of them had illuminated parts of myself. Maybe I hadn't needed to be in Ojai to make those realizations, but it certainly felt that I had landed in the right place at the right time. And the transformative journey I'd been on ever since had been an unrelenting one. I was still deeply in it.

My last encounter with Siobhan had been the most potent message of them all, and for whatever reason, I'd needed David to be a witness to that exchange. Ojai had certainly been an energetic portal for me; now, I understood that I'd gotten what I needed there, and there was no further reason to stay. Rather than viewing it as pushing me out, however, I saw it as showing me the way forward. The next step in my journey was to go deeper into these lessons—to ground my newfound awareness.

I hoped Santa Fe would be the right place to do that. I felt New Mexico calling to me. Maybe there I would learn how to embody the spiritual.

Part Three

HOMECOMING

Chapter 19

Reconnecting

The open road provided David and me an opportunity to connect in ways we'd hadn't for years, likely since living in Vietnam. In some ways, the real journey of our togetherness began only after our departure from Ojai.

En route to Santa Fe, we camped in Joshua Tree. I appreciated the groove we were in. I was driving the "sacred car," while David looked for the campground and helped organize the details of our plan as I drove.

When we arrived at the park, we took a short hike around the area where we were camping. We got ready for bed around seven. David pitched his tent next to my car, while I made a comfortable bed in the backseat. He had been car camping regularly in the past year, so he was comfortable with campsites and pitching tents. Similar to how he always guided me prior to an ayahuasca ceremony, he led me through the camping experience. I appreciated this "older brother" version of David, and truthfully, whether he understood it or not, I needed him. Even though I knew he was only a few feet away, the wide-open space of the desert frightened me.

"Don't knock on my door if you need anything," I told him. "It might scare me."

"Why don't we just assume that if someone knocks on your door, it'll be me," he said.

Even that little bit of reassurance helped me sleep more soundly that night.

From Joshua Tree, we headed for Flagstaff. David had booked us a cheap hotel online, but as we got closer, roadside signs warned of an imminent storm.

"Let's just drive straight to Santa Fe," I said. "It'll be around ten or twelve hours, but we can do it in one day."

David agreed, so we stopped only briefly in Flagstaff for coffee. He picked up a deck of tarot cards at the café before we left.

Back in the car, he took control of playing DJ. "What type of music do you want to listen to?" he asked.

"Something that reminds us of Vietnam," I suggested.

He found a playlist of songs that were popular in the early 2000s, and for the next couple of hours we sang the Backstreet Boys' "As Long As You Love Me" and other songs that brought us back to that time.

I'd almost forgotten how far back our history went. In many ways, he was the closest friend I had—and yet, in other ways, there had always been a distance between us that couldn't be closed. I remembered the time David approached me on the stairs in the place we shared in Saigon, early in our friendship, and said, "You know, I think we could be really close if you didn't have so many walls up around you."

I was twenty-two years old at that time and had never had anyone push through my boundaries and see through my protective layers. I hadn't even known anyone who wanted to try until I met David and he extended an invitation of friendship to me.

Now, as we drove toward Santa Fe, he said, "You know, Christina, one day we will know what all this means."

"Yes," I agreed. "Even though right now we have no clue how this adventure will unfold, one day it'll make sense to us why we went on this trip."

"Right now we have no idea," he reiterated, nodding.

We both had changed over the years, and I felt that we were at a beautiful moment in our tandem journey. On some level, we were returning to younger versions of ourselves—the selves who were following a whim, just because it felt like the right thing to do. But at the same time, we were embarking on this adventure with more fullness of perspective, now that we had lived more life than we'd had access to before. A combination of wisdom and youthfulness set the tone for this journey, and I couldn't imagine doing it without David. We had no idea what we were getting into, or what our time together would reveal, or where we would even end up—but at least we were together.

Six months before our road trip, I had attended a second plant medicine ceremony with David, once again led by Saanvi.

This ceremony took place on a plot of land two and half hours north of the Bay Area. Due to COVID protocols, it was also significantly smaller than the first had been, which I preferred. I planned to stay only one night.

Well before the ceremony took place, I began to see the signs that this time, lessons would unfold about my father. I had gone on a coffee date the week prior with a writing teacher. I shared with him what I was working on, and also my father's story, and he was deeply moved by my father's life. "Your father's entire life is about loss," he told me. "You need to get on a plane and visit him as soon as you can."

I thought about his words as the weekend approached. I went in feeling curious about what would unfold for me this time around.

I picked David up at his Oakland apartment to go to the ceremony. When he answered the door, he was in a frenzy.

"I'm running behind," he told me. "I'll explain in the car."

He had mentioned to me that he'd taken a caregiving job for an older couple for a few weeks to fill in for one of his friends who was going on vacation. Now he told me he'd received a call from his mom that morning, as he was packing, and she'd told him that his father would need to have open heart surgery in the coming weeks.

"My mom suggested that maybe I go back to help them out, but I already took on this other caregiving role," he said.

He was visibly shaken up over the dilemma of whether to stay or return to his family.

I didn't know what to say. I felt like I was the worst person to solicit for advice about family matters. A few years prior, my father had undergone heart surgery and hadn't even told me and my sister until after it was over. The image of him waking up alone in a hospital room after surgery was still heartbreaking for me.

I wanted to be there for David in the ways he was available to me. I didn't want us to continue living the dynamic where our relationship didn't feel balanced—but of course I didn't know how to tell him this. There is a fundamental difference between understanding something on a spiritual level and having the ability to relay that information in our human relationships—and I hadn't yet learned to bridge that gap. There was a chasm for me between the knowing and the doing.

"When my sister was in a coma, I was scared to go to Indiana to see her," I told him, trying to feel my way through to something that would help him. "I created all kinds of reasons why I couldn't go. I did it, though, and I was glad that I was there. It's hard to deal with these kinds of family health scares, especially with our parents as they age. It's scary. But the right decision will emerge."

I could see how the Grandmother energy was working in me

and with us around our families—and in particular our fathers—and I was afraid the energy of the ceremony might overwhelm me as it had the first time. I mentioned that fear to David.

"You know you can work with the medicine," David said. "You can be conscious of it and talk to the Grandmother energy. Just tell her if something is too much for you."

When we arrived at the ceremony, David was again warmly received by the familiar faces of his community. I was surprised to learn that three people had driven separately from New Mexico to attend.

David found Saanvi to speak to her about his father's health and the commitment he'd made to the elderly couple. After just ten or fifteen minutes speaking to her, he felt better and clearer about what to do. He would call the friend, tell her the situation, and return to help his parents. Days later, he told me that my sharing had also helped him make his decision. For perhaps the first time, I felt helpful to David.

This ceremony was a subtle experience compared to the first one, in which I had felt a great deal of separation and sadness. For most of the ceremony, I was outside, sitting on a swing near a little pond. Everything hit me softly, and gentle tears rolled down my face as I thought about my father.

My father had written a lot of his story in the years after my mother passed away. He'd attempted to fictionalize the characters, but I could see our family members clearly in his descriptions. He'd written with a mixture of emotion and intellect, although it had weighed heavily on the intellectual and factual side.

Through that book, *The Pink Lotus*, I had learned more about my father than I'd ever known, and now, during the ceremony, I saw his life flash before me like a movie. Experiencing this, I gained a deeper, more visceral understanding of what my father had endured—all of his losses—and why he could never express the pain he had suffered.

I began to see him in another light, and in turn I started to forgive him for not being able to be the father that I needed.

I had seen everything that I needed to see that evening.

After the first night, Saanvi approached me and asked me to stay. "Stay one more night," she said. "You're the only one of the group who is leaving."

But I knew it was time to go.

"There's a difference between running away from something and knowing when it's time to go," I told her. "This time, it's time for me to go home. I'm not running away."

I understood the lessons Grandmother had revealed to me in the ceremony, and I knew it was time for me to go home—just like David knew it was time for him to go home and support his parents.

Six months down the road, that theme—returning home—would become integral to our road trip. But we didn't know that yet.

Chapter 20

Forward Movement

It was dark and cold when we arrived in Santa Fe around nine o'clock. We couldn't see anything, and yet I felt the expansiveness of the land. There was also something about New Mexico that felt familiar—almost like home.

Jess had left the keys for us in the mailbox so we could check in after hours. She'd mentioned that there were three other people staying there—a couple from Colorado and a visiting college student whose father had rented a room for him for a week. She'd offered a great deal for two weeks, and an even better one for one month that I was ready to jump on. David and I had compromised, though, and agreed to book for just one week to start with; if we liked it, we could always stay longer.

When I opened the door to our room, I knew immediately that it was way too small. It had two twin beds and a tiny kitchenette. The aesthetic—deep tones of blue and purple, with a touch of golden yellow and Southwestern prints—suggested that we had arrived in a special place that had a deep reverence for the land. But even with those thoughtful touches, the size of the room and the two twin beds felt suffocating.

The Veil Between Two Worlds

Most places in Santa Fe were still closed, or open only for limited hours, due to COVID restrictions, so on our first day we stocked up on food from Trader Joe's that would last us a week, and in the subsequent days, David and I fell into a simple routine.

I woke up early and sat next to the fireplace in the common area to work in the mornings, or to write. The owner's father-in-law, a baker, would come in around seven with fresh-baked pastries for the overnight guests. I sometimes sat with the couple from Colorado at the wooden communal table and talked with them for a while; Jess and Rob, her friend who helped clean and do maintenance around the hotel, chatted with me here and there as well. I felt content there in that small space with friendly strangers who wanted to share bits of their lives.

David, in contrast, didn't seem to want to engage with anyone. Each morning, he pulled a card from his new tarot deck, and then went to check out a local hiking trail in the afternoon.

I felt I wanted to expand and connect, while David was contracting, wanting to stay inward. It was yet another difference between us, but I felt at ease with the fact that we were letting each other be.

By the time we'd been at the B&B for a week, sharing close quarters with David was starting to feel untenable. We had come to a decision to stay for one more week, but our energy had been intermingling in our tiny space, and I felt stagnant. He joked that sharing that room made him feel like we were in college. On some level, it was funny to me as well—but I wanted more space. That was one of the pulls of New Mexico, after all: the spaciousness.

I was working on an upcoming online event with Terra and her husband, Jack. The focus of the event was to help men and women find a middle ground—a place of mutual understanding—when faulty communication caused misunderstandings. Ironically, I wasn't living the lessons and messages that I wanted to impart to others. Being with David started to feel like I was sharing a space with someone I barely knew, not one of my closest friends. Truthfully, I wasn't used to spending so much time with anyone, and being in such a small space made me a bit claustrophobic.

Over the next few days, we began to take steps away from each other rather than communicating what we needed. We were slowly separating, our energies moving in different directions. True to my personality, I was thinking tangibly about next steps. I wanted to write more, not only for my personal project but also as a freelancer. I was also contemplating more seriously the idea of staying in Santa Fe permanently.

I got on Hinge just to get a quick assessment of what the dating pool was like here. "It's fun," I told David. "You should get online too." But he wasn't really interested in putting himself out there.

Oftentimes I noticed David staring out the window, and while he shared that he was processing deeper wounds and trauma passed down from generations, he didn't offer anything further. I didn't know how to access him—how to share that I, too, was going through a cathartic process. Neither of us seemed able to share with the other what we were going through, and we were clearly processing things very differently.

By this point, David and I had been together for two weeks total on our road trip. I decided it was time to put a little space between us.

One morning, I saw Rob cleaning one of the other rooms. When I asked if I could peek inside, I knew that I needed to stay there—alone, away from David and our tiny twin-size room. I booked the new room immediately, and I relished it. It had a kiva fireplace, a small sofa, a desk, a king-size bed, and a nicer shower. It felt luxurious compared to the small room David and I shared. More than the room, though, I valued my space.

The Veil Between Two Worlds

As I wrote and worked in my new room, a vision for myself of being in Santa Fe began to emerge. I could picture what I needed for the near-term future: a safe, ideally beautiful space where I could write. I didn't need more than that. I didn't even need a full kitchen. The traditional style of the casitas with the clay walls and natural colors inspired me, grounded me, and created a sense of safety for me. I wanted to stay on for months, not weeks, and I hoped that I could find the perfect writing casita. I hadn't visualized myself in a space in such a clear way since I'd first moved back to San Francisco and envisioned my apartment there. I knew then that something beautiful was emerging for me.

David, in contrast, didn't have a clear idea of what was next for him—and this bothered me. I felt he had so much potential, especially to help others in their own healing process. It wasn't my place, though, to push him along.

What I couldn't see clearly at that time was that my motorbike was a little ahead of his. He was where I'd been about a year and a half earlier, right when I left for Ojai. I was still reflecting and figuring things out, but I had at least come to the realization that Santa Fe was a place where I could ground for a bit. David, on the other hand, was basically looking only one to two weeks ahead. He had an online ceremony coming up with Saanvi's community. After that, he would go back to his parents' home in Phoenix on the weekend of the Lunar New Year for a Đám Giỗ for his grandparents, all of whom had passed within the first two weeks of February in different years. But he had nothing else planned beyond those two events.

A while back, I'd found a house for rent online that was just outside Santa Fe in a small town called Chupadero. I'd felt afraid of being out in the middle of the desert alone, so I'd turned it down, although the owner had assured me that the land would take care of me. Now I reached out to her and asked if by chance her home would be available to rent in March. Coincidentally, she was considering taking her family to Hawaii that month.

My plans were falling into place; a whole month in a comfortable home, a place where I would have time and space to formulate my next step, was just what I needed. The only challenge was getting David on board without allowing too much time to process, so we wouldn't lose the space.

One day I overheard David speaking to his mother, talking about their plans for the Lunar New Year.

"Why don't we celebrate on Saturday?" he suggested. "Let's check in with Mai and see if that works for her."

Listening to David, I wished I had a family that made holiday plans together and met frequently. I knew my father and I had unfinished business, and I thought I should use this opportunity to visit him. Selfishly, my preference was to stay in Santa Fe. But maybe, I thought, this was an opportunity for me to choose something different—to choose being with my father, rather than being alone—and further my growth.

While David was on the phone, I thought about the next steps. I could drive him back to Phoenix and spend a few days there, then fly to visit my dad. David could keep my car safe in Phoenix while I was away. We could reconvene back in New Mexico in March. I would fly there from Virginia and David could drive my car back.

As soon as David got off the phone, I made my pitch. He thought about it for a few minutes before agreeing to the first part. He said he needed time to assess whether it felt good for him, and to weigh whether my idea was being suggested by Eileen—my forceful, demanding side—or was coming from an authentic and grounded place. And, of course, he needed to see the home I'd lined up for March.

The Veil Between Two Worlds

In the end, we agreed it was time to go our separate ways for a few weeks, then reconvene in March. We both needed a break from one another.

The first time David coined the nickname Eileen, we were in Saigon, sharing a house. I had been hooking up with Karl, a German guy who lived with us, but when a new friend, Thi, moved in, Karl started spending a lot of time with her.

It infuriated me that they had a lot more in common than Karl and I did—enjoying the same music, chatting for hours—and David could see the fiery jealousy in my eyes. I always wanted to confront people when I felt that fierce anger, but even then, at the very beginning of our friendship, David cautioned me against it.

"It's like a whole different side of you," he told me one day. "You can be so warm and friendly, but then Eileen emerges and it's so scary."

It was that awareness and that ability to see me and accept me, even my worst side, that inspired in me a sense of loyalty to him.

A part of me had since come to understand that David was Eileen's first friend. Now, as we journeyed together nearly two decades later, I was learning to befriend Eileen as well. She was my unprocessed grief, my layer of protection that kept others from getting too close to me. She scared them away with her powerful emotions, and in fact she often scared me too.

I'd had time to sit with Eileen over the previous two years, and as I'd gotten to know her and started to allow her to express the grief underlying her anger, she'd softened. And I had softened as well. In the New Mexico desert, I came to the realization that it was time to let Eileen go, to shed that protective shield. I appreciated what she'd done for me, but I no longer needed her fierceness, and I knew now that only by letting her go or integrating her wounds within me would I be able to truly allow others in.

Chapter 21

Soul Family

On the way to David's parents' house, he shared something about them I'd never heard before. He said his parents, particularly his mother, were incredibly social and that throughout his childhood, they'd often thrown parties and had relatives come to stay with them for extended periods of time.

I thought again about how serendipitous it was that David's mom had met my uncle on a flight, and how that singular encounter had brought us together. That said, David and I were soul friends, and I knew we would have found our way to each other regardless of that interaction. Even the smallest coincidences seemed to reaffirm our connection: David's sister and my sister shared the same birthday; I shared a birthday with David's nephew; and David had the same birthday as Chase, my close friend who committed suicide. We were part of the same soul family. This I believed wholeheartedly, despite the distance I currently felt between us.

I had only met David's parents, Hương and Ed, once before, but I felt I knew them well; David had shared with me a lot about his family, and in particular his relationship with his mother, over the years. Much of David's healing was around wounds that showed up from his maternal line, and many of the challenges he described having with his mother were difficulties I imagined I would have faced with my own mother if she were still alive.

I wasn't surprised by how kind and friendly David's parents were when we arrived. It felt like we were two kids returning home from college rather than two forty-somethings on a road trip. When we walked in, they asked us all about our trip. It was comforting to feel how they had been awaiting our arrival.

Despite the fact that we were in Sunrise, Arizona—a suburb of Phoenix located a full two thousand miles away from my dad's home—David's parents' home reminded me of my father's place. It was clean, like his house. There were small reminders of Vietnam— little knickknacks and pieces of art. The kitchen was pristine. There was a rag on the floor and a stool in the middle of the floor.

"This looks like my dad's kitchen," I told David's mom. "He has a stool in the middle of the floor and a rag as well. Why do you have a stool here?"

"So I can sit and watch the TV while I wash dishes here at the sink," she responded.

There was a certain pragmatism in her answer that felt very Vietnamese. I knew that, in my father's case, the stool was there so he could look outside the window at the persimmon tree he had planted—also, very likely, as he washed the dishes.

I imagined, too, that if I looked in the fridge or in the cabinets, there would be similar condiments and Vietnamese food that my father would have as well. Srichacha. Maggi. Chả lụa.

I felt at home. It was a soothing sensation.

I felt connected to David's mother, Hương. I often appreciated my friends' mothers, and women who were around my mother's age in general—an affinity I attributed to my motherlessness.

Many of the complaints my Vietnamese friends had about their mothers revolved around their mothers not doing "the work." This usually meant unraveling their wounds and traumas of the war and the dynamics of their families. David would often say that his mother wasn't aware of her own trauma and how she played it out in her life.

I criticized my father for this as well, but I was also coming to the realization that their generation was different from ours. They had different wounds to heal, and this was part of our collective evolution. When people of our parents' generation fled Vietnam and immigrated to the United States, their focus was on survival—on making things work in this country for themselves and their families. Our lives and struggles were different. We were building and healing off the foundation they had created for us.

Hương and I bonded over our shared love for David. She was curious about what I was doing as well, and how I had managed to take the time off to go on the road trip. I explained to her that I was writing and working on freelance projects. She made the observation that I was on calls or working every day, but David did not seem to be working toward anything. He had not told them about his medicine path and the deep spiritual work he was doing with Saanvi's community, and it was not my place to share that information—not in any specific way, at least.

When we had a moment alone, Hương asked me, "What do you think is wrong with David? Do you think he's okay? Is he depressed?"

I had my concerns about David, but I didn't want to get into those details with his mother.

"I think he's fine," I said carefully. "He'll figure it out."

"But he's never been this way," she told me. "He's always been so focused on everything that he wanted in his life, and he achieved it. Now, he doesn't seem to be interested in anything."

"You know the book *Siddhartha*, the story of Buddha's journey?" I asked.

She nodded. "Yes, I do."

"That's what David's doing," I tried to explain. "He is doing deep work—spiritual work—and that is his purpose right now."

Hương let out a big sigh of relief. "Ohhh, like *Siddhartha*."

I could tell that I had penetrated one layer of her awareness, but the deeper conversation and explanation would need to come from David, on his own terms.

David and I hadn't spoken about what was going on with him. I was afraid to ask because I didn't want to put him on the defensive. We had secrets between us. I knew this. He had his own private things going on, and there was something I hadn't told him: I was searching for a permanent place to stay in Santa Fe, and I wasn't interested in sharing a place. I needed to be alone.

I responded to a post on Craigslist about a short-term studio casita for rent on a historic road in Santa Fe. I fell in love with the place immediately when I saw the pictures. The one-room casita had wooden floors and high ceilings—they seemed to be ten to twelve feet high—with naked wood beams. The tall front door looked as if it had come from medieval times. There was a small kitchenette hidden behind painted doors. It was charming, well-lit, and a five-minute walk from Canyon Road, the one-mile street filled with art galleries. I wanted to take it immediately, for however long the landlord would allow me to be there. She'd offered it for three to five months in the posting.

The posting listed March as the start date; I called the number and said that I could take the casita starting in April. She said there was a woman who might want it for just one month; she would confirm with her and call me back.

David and I hadn't discussed what would happen after we shared the house in March—but when the woman called me back and told me that I could have the place, I said yes without hesitation. David would need to take his time with any decision; this casita required action.

Once I got off the phone, I dashed to the kitchen to show Hương the pictures of the place.

"I'm going to stay in Santa Fe longer," I told her excitedly. "I found a place."

"I'm so happy for you," she responded. "Seems like you really like it there."

I was starting to put a foot down in Santa Fe, and yet that came with a sense that I was moving further away from David.

David smiled at me from his seat at the kitchen table and said. "I'm happy you found a place."

I knew but didn't want to admit that I should have talked to him about this plan first—not for permission, but simply to keep him informed. But I was too excited and too focused on my own journey to see the tinge of disappointment in David's eyes when I shared my news. It wouldn't be until a few weeks later that he would share with me that he was genuinely happy that I'd decided to stay in Santa Fe longer and that I'd found a place, but he thought I could have chosen a better way to broach the topic with him.

We'd always differed in the pace of our approach to decisions and decision-making. That difference had also always been a point of contention between us. But this time around, David's slow-moving nature was wearying—and, frankly, anxiety-inducing. I also knew I had a talent for finding beautiful spaces and developing an amicable relationship with landlords. Just as I was growing to accept and understand Eileen, I could also feel an appreciation for the fast-moving side of myself that sensed intuitively that I needed to find a permanent home, that I needed stability. I wanted to put down roots and develop the next phase of my life, and the urgency I felt around doing it was strong—so strong that even my friendship with David couldn't get in the way.

The Veil Between Two Worlds

✦✦

On the last evening I spent at David's parents' home, we ended up talking about David's childhood friends who used to come over to their place.

"What happened to Lucy?" David's father asked him.

"I don't know," he said, shaking his head. He looked at me and explained, "Lucy was a Korean girl who used to come over to our house every day after school."

"It was clear that there was something going on in her house," Ed said. "She would just come over and knock on the door, and then sit on the couch and watch TV. She was the sweetest girl, and didn't seem to need anything but a safe place to sit."

The image of Lucy, a teenage girl who needed a safe refuge, a home away from home, resonated with me. I saw myself as a teenager with that very same need, and I wished for the younger version of myself that I could have had David as a friend then, and David's parents' home as a place to escape to.

I realized something about healing in that moment—that it's not always in the moment, and that it's often not linear. Just hearing about Lucy and imagining the comfort she felt in Hương and Ed's home healed a part of my younger self.

In spite of our current disconnect, I felt grateful to have David as a soul friend. I could see that every part of our road trip had a purpose—a healing element—and I knew then that I had the courage to sit through whatever would come up for me when I returned to my father's house.

Chapter 22

Continuation

Although I yearned to return to the spaciousness of New Mexico–a far cry from the cookie-cutter Northern Virginia neighborhood where my father lived–I knew I had to follow through on my plans to visit him.

The silence of my father's home had once haunted me, but now the wounds of the past had come into my consciousness; instead of allowing myself to be controlled by them, I was aware of them. I'd once heard that the universe repeatedly gives us the same challenges, although they might look different on the outside, until we heal them. This was certainly true in my life. My recent journey had given me the courage to stay with my father for two weeks–the longest period of time I'd spent with him since college.

It felt like a natural continuation from David's parents' home to my father's place, if for no other reason than the fact that Lunar New Year had just passed and the festive atmosphere was visible in both homes. My father had mums and a plate full of dragon fruit, pineapple, and tangerines on his dining room table, which was where I usually sat and worked. When I peered in the fridge, he had

The Veil Between Two Worlds

bánh tét, a Lunar New Year delicacy, and chocolate-covered strawber-
ries, too, since Valentine's Day had recently passed (coincidentally,
Hương had purchased those as a gift for her husband as well). Then
there was the familiar stool in the middle of the kitchen—which, as
I remembered Hương and Ed's home and their story about Lucy,
provided me with a sense of groundedness.

When I arrived at my father's home, I always scanned it thor-
oughly—odd, since he rarely changed anything, and I had more or
less memorized the contents, but it was an old habit. As I surveyed
the house, I saw pieces of all the women who had been part of his
life: my mother; his second wife, Liên; and Thảo, his current girlfriend. Without these women, I wasn't sure if I would have ever
been able to connect with my father. Each one had been a direct line
of communication to him for me, despite having their own problems
connecting with him.

In my bedroom and in the kitchen, I could feel my mother's
presence. Every time I returned there, I wondered, *What would it
have been like had she lived? Would our family have become something different?* Five of her sweaters were still folded in my dresser, her yellow
raincoat still hung in the closet, and a crocheted blanket she'd made
when she was sick was folded at the end of the bed. Even though my
father barely used the kitchen, he never discarded her kitchenware,
from the KitchenAid mixer to the Marimekko mugs, Corningware
baking dishes, and holiday plates that lined the top shelf above the
kitchen cabinets.

The small lanterns I'd purchased in Hội An, Vietnam, when he
was still married to Liên hung from the banister above the foyer.
Liên was a doctor and also an artist. Her presence lingered in
his house, too, in the more decorative items, like the simple faux
arrangements in the enclave above the stairs and on the entryway
table. In the corner of the dining room on a wooden table next to
the window sat a flowering orchid. A piece of paper with a flower

painted on it was taped to the side. Written in Liên's handwriting, it said: *If you love something, let it go. If it comes back to you, then it's yours forever. If it doesn't, then it was never yours to begin with.*

Fifteen years after their relationship had ended, that piece of paper was still taped on the table, and I felt Liên's presence most strongly there. Had Liên been his one true love?

On the kitchen counter next to the phone, there were a few photos of Thảo and my father: one at a Vietnamese community event, one in New Orleans, and another of them whitewater rafting with friends in Tennessee. On the mantel, alongside my father's sailboat figurines, was a picture of them at the beach. Those images evoked regret in me for not having spent more time with my father over the years. Every time I opened the fridge and saw Vietnamese food, I was reminded of Thảo, as I was certain that my father wouldn't have prepared what was in there by himself.

I was grateful for Thảo. While they didn't live together, I knew she phoned him daily to check in on him. When my sister was in a coma, I'd become closer to her, and on every visit thereafter, my appreciation for her had grown. She was a Buddhist, and she had a gentle way with me and my father.

A few years earlier, before my sister's coma, Thảo had taken me shopping at Tysons Corner, a large shopping mall in Northern Virginia. She was always immaculately put together and loved to shop. She couldn't help but encourage me to buy clothes and accessories for myself. I understood that she would have loved to tell me directly that I should pay more attention to how I looked, but instead, as we shopped, she restricted herself to pointing out various items, from sweaters to dresses, that she thought would look nice on me.

She told me about how she'd met my father at an event years before. After first seeing him, she'd asked around about him. Someone told her about his divorce–that it was the main reason he'd left Indiana, and that it had been hard for him.

The Veil Between Two Worlds

It was heartbreaking for me to think of him at that event—a man who barely spoke, trying so hard to be social. It struck me how little I had been there for him throughout my life.

"Your father, he never says anything to me," Thảo shared while we shopped. "He barely talks to me. But I love him, so I try to understand him."

Liên had confided similarly in me after their divorce, only a few years after my graduation from college. She'd flown to North Carolina, where I was staying for the summer, for a visit, and we spoke about my father. But rather than being a civil conversation, it was a fight. There were too many emotions unspoken between us, and it didn't surprise me that the end of their relationship was explosive for the two of us. Both my sister and I felt that she and my father had begun their relationship too soon after our mother had passed, and I was often upset with Liên because I felt she favored me over my sister.

One moment from that conversation with Liên had lodged itself in my head: "You know how you always complained that your father doesn't talk to you? Well, he doesn't talk to me either."

As I reflected on these conversations, I understood that there was a bond between the women my father loved and me. We knew what it was like, and how hard it was, to love a man who barely spoke—and in spite of our differences, this tied us together, sometimes well beyond their relationship with my father.

Every day during my visit, my father left food for me on the kitchen table. This was his love language. Sometimes, in the evenings, we'd go to a local Thai restaurant with Thảo, or she would bring over Vietnamese sandwiches or *bánh cuốn,* my favorite Vietnamese dish. I would have been satisfied eating leftovers, which were bountiful, but every day, without fail, a new dish appeared. Sometimes it would be something simple that my father had prepared himself by heating up leftovers and adding vegetables so it became another dish. One day, there was a large pot of *bún riêu*, crab noodle soup. Another evening, fresh king crab legs and four lobster tails appeared on a plate on the table.

At times, I wanted to tell my father that the food felt excessive—that I didn't even have time to eat one dish before another one was there on the table. I bit my tongue, though, because I knew it was the only way he knew to show his love, and I couldn't bear to hurt his feelings.

I thought back to the time after my mother's death when my sister had already left for college and only my father and I were in the home. While we barely interacted, often not seeing each other for days, there was always food for me. For a period of time, I only wanted to eat Chex cereal. There was a limited-edition Chex with graham crackers that I devoured. My father noticed; I came home one day to find ten boxes of the stuff in our cupboards.

I once read a story my father wrote about how, when he was a child in Vietnam, he was sent to stay with his grandmother on a longan orchard in Vũng Tàu, a coastal town about sixty miles from Saigon. For a long time, he didn't understand why his mother sent him away; only later did someone explain that there had been a trade so that another family member could attend school in Saigon.

One day, my father wrote, a beautiful woman came to visit his grandmother. She took him shopping with her and to the beach. A sadness overtook my father when he realized that the woman made him miss his mother, and her maternal love.

That story always stood out in my mind, but it took years after reading it for me to understand that there was no way my father could have given to me what he had not had himself: a consistent, nurturing maternal love. All these years, I'd wanted him to be a mother to me, rather than accepting that he could never be that for me. Now I was beginning to understand that he offered something different.

The Veil Between Two Worlds

I didn't know how to show my father my love, either. Words had never been a common language between us, so instead I attempted to make his home more comfortable and decorated—something I knew how to do well. I bought a new electric tea kettle. I organized his kitchen cabinets and dusted the chandelier and in front of the fireplace—two places that felt forgotten. I lit candles to make the home feel more cozy at night.

The next time Thảo came over to shop, we went to Costco and HomeGoods, and I suggested that we buy a rug for the family room and rearrange the furniture so it felt more cozy. She was on board, and when we spoke to my father, he agreed too. Shortly thereafter, they asked me to help decorate the living room. I rearranged the pillows and turned on more lamps in the evening, which created a sense of warmth—the very thing my father's house had been missing. Something maybe only a woman's love and nurturing could bring to his home.

Slowly, I started to feel that my father, Thảo, and I were a unit. It wasn't the kind of unit I might have wished for, and yet I did feel comforted by their presence and glad to be spending this time with them.

During the two weeks I was in Virginia, I saw my therapist once over Zoom. I told him that I'd woken up for days in a row with puffy eyes and that I was crying in my sleep. He told me my subconscious was healing for me, and whatever I was going through was almost too much for my conscious brain to understand. He assured me that I was working through things in my sleep.

"Your psyche has been protecting you from the deep wells of grief that had lived within you for so long," he said. "Now it's letting some of that grief out."

He then explained to me that I seemed to cope with grief in three ways: overexcitement, which was almost a bypassing of the emotions and experiences; leaving or dismissing the experience; or finding ways in which people were flawed.

"You were overwhelmed by your mother, your father was impenetrable, and your sister was numb. You see people in these categories, and yet there's an entire spectrum of being, and so many ways in which you can relate to people."

I was shocked and humbled by his astuteness. I knew I wanted a different future for myself—one that wasn't isolated, one in which I could be an empowered and independent woman who chose to live fully, who chose not to run away or live in fear.

I was ready to heal and feel a wider range of emotions—ready to arrive at a deeper place of understanding about myself, my upbringing, and my future path.

I started to feel clarity about my life and next steps. I sent an email to Chloe telling her I was ready to transfer the lease over to her. I knew that for at least the next four or five months I would be in Santa Fe; I had secured the casita for that time. Beyond that, I could let things unfold. I didn't have a concrete plan, and I didn't really want one.

While I was in Virginia, I met Rachel, a therapist and a mutual friend of David and mine, for coffee. We began by speaking about how the pandemic had been for us but ended up focused on David, which was perhaps unsurprising, given how much time I'd spent with him in the previous month. I needed to vent and to speak to someone who knew David but was also cognizant of the way our wounds and patterns reappear in our lives, and Rachel was the perfect person for that conversation.

"I don't know what he's doing," I said. "I don't know why he's not trying to do anything."

"You can't take care of him, Christina," she told me. "You aren't responsible for him, and he needs to figure it out. Are you paying for everything?"

"No," I assured her. "We're splitting everything. But I do a lot of the coordination."

I felt simultaneously guilty for speaking about David but also relieved to get things off my chest. I wanted him to find a job, to fully express his purpose. I knew the spiritual community was giving his life meaning, but I wanted to see him use his gifts.

And yet, it wasn't my place to pressure him about that.

I'd become more possessive about my car, which was probably a manifestation of my desire to create distance between us. He was doing me a favor by driving it back to New Mexico, but I thought about the fact that we would soon be living somewhere located fifteen minutes outside of Santa Fe, and I didn't like the thought of having to share my car with him.

Eileen reared her head; I sent him a text message suggesting that he think about renting a car when we got back to Santa Fe, since he might want to go on trips and I would be staying on for longer than he would.

He wrote back non-defensively: *That makes sense. I'll look into it.*

That only made me feel more guilty—for lashing out at him, for being upset with him for not matching me lockstep in our parallel journeys. Although I was doing better at feeling my emotions, I still wasn't ready to understand that what I was feeling with David was loss, and that loss tapped into a well of grief so deep that it seemed to know no bottom.

Chapter 23

An Invitation
to the Land

When I returned to Santa Fe after leaving Virginia, New Mexico welcomed me in a way I had never felt before. Perhaps it was the timing of my sojourn there, but I believe it had more to do with the fact that I was returning to the home within myself after reconciling so much that had not been healed in relation to my father. The desert, with its endless space, created a feeling of heart-expansiveness within me.

The house David and I had rented was beautiful—a quintessential adobe home with stucco walls that had been tastefully decorated by its multitalented owners, a jewelry designer and a woodworker. I loved the minimalist, natural decor throughout and the fact that they had a room dedicated to meditation. The home was textured—beautiful ceramic mugs, rattan seat cushions, and wood pieces that appeared to be handcrafted by the owner, including a desk the woodworker had made from scratch for me in the weeks before I moved in after I mentioned that I would need one for writing. There were also two cats, and one rather large but super friendly dog,

Palo, that roamed the property. Two more structures, a small casita and a woodworking studio, stood behind the house.

Even though David and I were sharing a beautiful and spacious home, I felt a coldness toward him that I wasn't good at concealing. It came over me when I couldn't express what I wanted to say. It didn't make sense to me on a conscious level: David was one of my closest friends, we'd been traveling together since the beginning of the year, and we'd been on a parallel path for nearly two decades. But this distance between us was like an unbridgeable gulf, and it upset me. On the one hand, I was moving forward with a lot of clarity: I was determined to stay in Santa Fe, and now part of the equation—the housing situation for after March—was already resolved. But that wasn't enough for me; I wanted David to be riding alongside me, not ahead of me or behind me.

I had questions for him: *How are you really doing, David? Are you okay?* I wanted to tell him I was worried about him. I wanted to share my trepidation and excitement about what was coming up for me.

Instead, I just gave him the cold shoulder.

He'd listened and moved quickly on my suggestion for him to have his own means of transportation. But that translated into him buying a car, which he wanted to go back to Phoenix to do, and now he said he wasn't sure he'd even make it back to Santa Fe after he bought it. "It depends on when I get the car and how much time is left on the lease," he told me.

I was shocked at this. It meant I would be in the rental home alone for an extended period of time—something I wasn't mentally prepared to do. I was invested in him being there with me, and I told him that I hoped after he bought the car he would return for the remaining few weeks. I did want to be there *with* him—because I wanted to spend time with him and, selfishly, because I still wasn't comfortable sleeping in the middle of the New Mexico desert alone.

Maybe if I could have been more vulnerable with him, I could have asked for what I really needed. I wanted him close, but I was pushing him away. I was still stuck in my patterns. The good news was that I was feeling more of my emotions—but there was still a big gap between my awareness and my actions. I was much more conscious of the wounds, but words could still sometimes get trapped in my throat.

In the few days that we shared the house before David returned to Phoenix to buy his car, we lived separate lives. This didn't feel much different from how we'd been at the bed and breakfast, but I'd thought sharing a home with a kitchen and having our separate rooms would allow us to have our space and also remain connected. I was wrong. We each just did our own thing. Later, I would understand how attuned David was to what I needed in the moment, and that he was giving me the space to settle into my new life. But as it was happening, I felt disconnected from David and upset with myself that I was being so avoidant.

One afternoon when we were both home, David came out of his room for a moment, and I could see he was upset. His eyes were puffy, and he was clearly trying to avoid me. Later in the evening, our paths crossed in the kitchen, and he told me that he'd connected with someone online. He told me that he had gotten on the online dating apps while I was away, and there was one person in particular with whom he felt a connection—someone who had also recently moved to Santa Fe.

"I finally connected with someone, Christina. And now he's not sure if he wants to meet." David sighed. "I know whatever I'm feeling is not about this person being uncertain about meeting me, though; it's more about going deeper into what this wound actually is about."

We often talked about my wounds, so I appreciated it when

David spoke about his, which was less common. I knew he wanted a connection that felt reciprocal. I knew from my own journey, too, that it could take a lot of time to work through the wounds that come up in dating.

"I understand—I really do," I told him. "I'm glad you're connecting with people. And I hope that you do end up meeting this guy here."

There was so much more I wanted to say. So much more that I wanted for him. So much that he could offer people that I felt he withheld. I knew the same was true for me—that my coldness was my own way of withholding. I was seeing parts of myself in him. He was a sacred mirror to me, as he always had been.

I felt convinced that I wouldn't be able to sleep when David returned to Phoenix. A part of me was relieved that I would have that time alone, as I didn't want to feel the energy of another person around me, and yet I was growing used to this idea of being someone who could embrace solitude but also be connected to others in a healthy manner.

The first night I spent alone in the house, every creak woke me up. I left the living room light on, as well as all the outdoor lights and a small lamp in my bedroom. I imagined there was someone outside the house; I felt sure that if I looked up, I would see someone peering in through the curtainless window. I heard coyotes howling in the distance, and even that felt threatening to me.

Palo, the owner's dog, normally slept outside, but that second night I brought him in to sleep in the living room. Comforted by the fact that another living being was sharing the house with me, I was able to sleep through the night.

I was safe. I was home.

The environment brought me into a natural creative state, so much so that I felt called to write in the middle of the night to express what was coming through me. Other realizations crystallized, like the many ways my ideas of my family kept me separated from love—not only romantic love but almost every type of loving relationship. I remembered all the friendships I'd let go of in the last few years because I believed those friends couldn't understand what I was going through and wouldn't support me. My therapist had mentioned to me a month earlier that my ego was preventing me from feeling grief—that this was where the walls came up. I didn't want to keep living in a world of separation. But the change wasn't going to happen on its own.

One morning, I woke up to find that fresh snow had fallen the night before. I looked out the living room window, and my attention was arrested by the mountain in the distance. Feeling surrounded by a nourishing energy I had not experienced before, I stared at the mountain and the sublimely beautiful snow and felt a deep understanding of my mother, my father, my sister, and everyone in my life that I loved. I felt what we were all seeking—connection and love—and I recognized something profound: for many of us, the purpose of life is to be on a journey of self-love, and then to see how that love of self allows us to love others in a deeper way.

Finally, I was close to the land and felt a connection to it. I'd heeded the message I'd received earlier in the year that had compelled me to sleep on the floor in my Noe Valley apartment. I understood what I was being called to do and what it meant to feel firmly rooted in one place, protected by natural surroundings. I saw the mountain as a metaphor for Mother Earth—and felt intuitively that Mother Earth's love was the deepest example of love there could be.

I didn't yet know how to articulate these realizations that were coming to me, or how they would play out in my life. But I thought it was enough for now to hold as true what the owner of the house had told me about the land—that it would take care of me and would help me feel safe.

∷

Chapter 24

A Ceremonial Ending

D avid returned with his newly purchased car after a few days. More than anything, I was eager to get us to the end of the month. While he was away, I'd concocted a plan of how we would end our road trip journey together. A woman, Nova, I knew from an online business group had recently moved to Albuquerque from Los Angeles. She was a sound healer and women's coach who was just beginning to go deeper with the spiritual communities in New Mexico. I had received an email from her one morning telling me that her friend, a healer from South America, was going to be in town for a month and that they were planning to host a series of plant medicine ceremonies with mushrooms at her home in Albuquerque. I suggested to David that we attend together as a way of closing our time together in New Mexico. Since we'd started this journey with a ceremony, it felt appropriate to end it with one too.

David was wary of other communities and ceremonies, so he asked to speak to Nova first, before committing.

I arranged for us to meet Nova and her partner for lunch in Santa Fe in late March.

✴✴

When we met for lunch, Nova raved about the shaman, Diego, who would be leading the ceremony.

"He's just so full of love," she gushed. "Pure, unconditional love. You will both love him. Everyone who meets Diego loves him."

I didn't particularly desire another ceremony. The truth was that I wanted this experience more for David than for myself.

Nova was convincing, however, mentioning that Diego was also a musician and would be singing during the ceremony. "It's going to be so special," she told us.

"I'll go," I said to Nova. "I just have to figure out which date."

"I'm in as well," David chimed in.

The closing of our time together began to take shape. David planned to car camp in northern New Mexico and southern Colorado for the week and half before the ceremony. Then, after the ceremony, he'd head back to the Bay Area.

I was eager to get situated in my new casita and begin my Santa Fe life. Our journey was coming to a close, and even though I couldn't grasp what it all meant, having closure in this way felt important and meaningful. I was thrilled that we would be parting ways from each other on grounded, even sacred, terms.

It was the beginning of April, and the ceremony was two weeks away. I prepared for my move into the casita, and David got ready for his two week car camping adventure. Before he left, he helped me bring my minimal belongings to the casita.

It was even more beautiful than the pictures had promised. The property was gated, and there was a little yard area and some gravel steps leading up to it that made it feel secluded and safe.

After assessing the place, I asked David to help me move the furniture around. I wanted the table to be in the center of the room because I was determined to make this period of my life about my writing, and I wanted my space to reflect that. In the lease, I'd noticed there was an additional fee for overnight guests. I treasured the place so much that I didn't want to upset the landlord, so I didn't let David stay with me that evening. I was moving toward grounding, stabilizing myself in one place, while David was still embarking on an adventure. It was a distinct shift and moment of change for me and David: our paths were diverging.

I relished living in a place on my own, and a beautiful casita nonetheless. I learned that the property was owned by an artist, Fremont Ellis, who'd moved to Santa Fe in the 1920s and, together with four friends, had created a collective of artists known as Los Cinco Pintores. Since arriving in Santa Fe, I'd become familiar with the stories of female artists like Georgia O'Keeffe and Judy Chicago, who had found comfort and inspiration in New Mexico. I'd also discovered that in the first half of the twentieth century, New Mexico had been a haven for pioneering women who wanted to escape the social restrictions of the East Coast cities. There was a long history of artists and pioneers who had found inspiration in New Mexico's rich landscape and spiritual life. I sensed the creative energy that seemed to live in the spirit of my home, and the land in general, and it felt warm and welcoming.

The next morning, I walked around my neighborhood in the Eastside of Santa Fe—which, I now knew, was one of the most coveted neighborhoods in the town. I met a woman walking her dog. She told me she was visiting from Oklahoma and said she and her girlfriend visited Santa Fe every year and stayed for a week. She raved about Santa Fe—the natural beauty, the art and culture, the sheer magic. Although she loved it, she confided, she would never want to live there because she felt Santa Fe would lose its luster if she experienced it daily. I didn't agree; in fact, when she said that, something within me wanted to prove her wrong. I believed it was possible to create and feel magic daily.

After parting ways with my new acquaintance, I looked at the trees alongside Alameda Street and listened to the flowing sound of the Santa Fe River, and I realized I needed to stay longer, beyond the three months of my lease. A deep desire arose within me to experience all the seasons in New Mexico and to see if the magic could be with me year-round.

In that moment, for the first time of the entire journey, I prayed to the land, asking if there could be a way for me to stay.

)(

Chapter 25

Grandmother Returns

I n mid-April, David returned so we could attend the ceremony together. I had my reservations, and I'd later learn that he did as well.

We were both a little frenetic when he came to my casita to pick me up. Our energy was not aligned. For the first time, I hadn't followed the recommended diet prior to a ceremony.

On the drive to Albuquerque, David spoke about the people he'd met on his car camping with an excitement that I'd rarely witnessed in him. He'd even had a short romantic fling, which he described as a heartwarming and tender experience.

"They were so kind to me, Christina," he said, beaming. "Some of these places where I stayed were small towns, and people made an effort to tell me about the secret places that most wouldn't have access to. It was so special."

I was happy for him, and I told him so. I felt lighter as we made the one-hour drive from Santa Fe to the ceremony and continued to share more about our lives in a way we hadn't in the previous months. I told him about how much I loved the casita and the neighborhood. I shared with him some of the imbalances I felt in my life, how I was contemplating closing my women's Facebook group, and that my close relationships with women, specifically Terra, had been shifting. She wanted me to do more writing for her business, but I wasn't interested in working on those projects at the moment.

"You two are so close—you'll figure it out," he assured me.

I knew he was right, and knowing that whatever had been going on between us would be resolved, too, gave me great fortitude.

The heaviness and distance that had in many ways defined our road trip was no longer there, and I felt a huge sense of relief.

As we did before each ceremony, we stopped at the grocery store to pick up fruit to share with the group. Nova had requested that we each bring a chocolate bar to the ceremony as well; I thought that was a bit odd, but grabbed one as instructed.

A noticeable sense of fun and lightness had reemerged between David and me, and I was so grateful. The adventurous spirit we had started with on our journey was present once again.

When we arrived at the house Nova had rented, where the ceremony was taking place, there were only a few people there: Nova, Diego, and another woman. As Nova gave us a tour, she mentioned that the house was owned by a set designer. A one-story home with three bedrooms, it was cozy and well-decorated. We were fortunate that not many people were attending the ceremony, and David and I were able to share a single bedroom.

In the living room where the ceremony was taking place, flamingo wallpaper overwhelmed the walls—a surprising choice for a ranch-style home in the middle of Albuquerque. The whole house did indeed feel like a set. The decorations made me feel as if we were in Los Angeles.

David and I were initially aloof with Nova and the woman from

Los Angeles. I wasn't in the mood to engage. Still, the woman tried, and seeing her effort, I pulled myself out of my protective armor.

"So, how did you guys meet?" she asked.

"We've been friends for nearly two decades," I said.

"So you're not together?"

"No, we're not together. Just good friends."

I didn't probe deeper into her story. I had a feeling, given her immediate focus on our relationship status, that she was dealing with relationship issues—which felt too close to my own recent journey.

David spent most of the time outside before returning to the room where the ceremony took place. We were both distracted and disengaged. I could sense that, and I'm sure the others could too.

As Diego prepared the ceremony, each of us pulled a tarot card. At one point, as Diego was preparing the "sacred fire," he asked David to help him. I knew David well enough to read his reluctance, but he went ahead and did so.

The ceremony wasn't set up like Saanvi's, in the sense that it wasn't at all formal; nobody offered up even rough guidelines for the evening. But I hadn't been to any other ceremonies except for Saanvi's, so I had no frame of reference besides what I'd seen her do.

On the dining room table, I saw the ceremonial mushrooms placed in a martini glass with pieces of chocolate on top of them. I don't know what I'd thought the chocolate was for prior to this, but I felt judgment rising in me as I looked at the chocolate there, simply placed in a glass with the mushrooms.

I looked down at the little mushroom caps and stems in my glass and knew immediately that it was too many for me—I only needed a small amount to feel the effect—but I overrode what I knew and ate everything. David was sitting next to me on the sofa, but I didn't pay attention to what he was doing.

It didn't take long for the effect of the mushrooms to hit me. Hard.

Diego sang one song on repeat. Nova had sent us some of his songs before we attended the ceremony. I hadn't listened to them, but David had, and it had reinforced his decision to attend. Now, however, Diego just danced around the small room in front of the fire singing the same verse repeatedly: *Cleaning, clearing the energy. I am cleaning, clearing the energy.*

I was still conscious enough to see that David had left the room. I was becoming more and more affected by the mushrooms, so I started to pay less and less attention to Nova and the other woman. By this point, Diego had taken off his shirt and was dancing in front of the fire. He was not setting the energy of the room but rather having his own experience.

A few minutes later, I noticed David had returned and was sitting next to me on the sofa again.

He whispered to me, "This isn't real."

I was confused. "What do you mean, this isn't real?"

"This isn't a real ceremony," he said. "I'm hanging out in my room if you want to join me."

All of a sudden, the absurdity of the situation struck me. I started to giggle. "Let's go," I agreed.

When we got to our room, David explained to me all the things that were off about the ceremony and how it wasn't set up in a sacred fashion.

"What are we doing here?" he asked.

"I have no idea," I told him.

As the mushrooms started to impact me more strongly, another energy overtook me.

We heard a woman wailing in the other room. I wasn't sure if it was Nova or the woman from L.A., but I told David we should ignore her, then started to speak of the sadness of Mother Earth.

The mushrooms were impacting David as well, though his focus was on why we were there—how we'd ended up in this fake ceremony.

The Veil Between Two Worlds

"Don't worry about that, or the people in the other room," I told him. "We have to focus on how much Mother Earth does for us and how much we take advantage of her. She's there for us. She takes care of us. Gives us land and shelter and food. And we just take and take and take. It's so sad, David."

"How did this happen?" he said. "We should call the police. This is really wrong, Christina."

"Just focus, David," I insisted. "It's really sad what happens to humans. Don't listen to the woman out there, but it's also a lesson of the suffering felt by humans. There's so much separation in the world, and this is what causes conflict–the suffering of existence. But we must always remember Mother Earth. We have to take care of her and be disciplined in our lives."

"Christina, where is this coming from?" he asked.

I could see that David was truly upset, and I was startled out of my train of thought about Mother Earth.

"How did I end up here?" he asked. "How did I end up here at this age?"

I knew he was speaking about the deeper wound he'd been working on for a while now–maybe for our whole trip, maybe for much longer. I wanted to delve deeper with him, but we were interrupted by a knock on our door.

"Guys, are you okay?" It was Nova. "Do you want to come back to the ceremony?"

"We're fine," David answered.

We took a moment, then agreed to go back out to join the others.

When we walked back into the living room, we saw that Nova's partner, who'd come to the ceremony late because he was still working, was sitting on the floor next to Nova. The woman from Los Angeles was lying on the ground.

Diego, who was sitting on a sofa, kept insisting that I move close to him. "Come here, Christina," he said more than once.

I shook my head. "I'm fine here." I was sitting on the ground. David was right behind me in a chair.

"You can, Christina," Diego said. "You can sit here."

His voice was insistent, pushy. I was grateful that David was behind me.

Diego got up and came and kneeled next to me, which also made me uncomfortable. I was too high from the mushrooms to read the situation appropriately, but instinctively I didn't like what was unfolding.

"She's fine," David said. "She doesn't want to sit next to you."

I looked at David and motioned him to come with me to another room. We rose and left the living room.

I looked into David's eyes. "Remember this moment," I said. "Be a witness to how Diego approached me and what it can be like for women."

"I will remember," he assured me.

Suddenly, we were on the same page. Mostly, we no longer wanted to be there.

"We have to leave, Christina," David said. "They basically just drugged us."

Slowly, we moved into a place where we felt some urgency to leave.

"Let's put our things together and go," I agreed.

I was surprised by David's emotion, and his anger. As we walked out, David said to Nova and Diego, "This isn't a real ceremony. What you guys are doing isn't real."

"We're leaving," I explained. "We don't feel safe here. The ceremony doesn't feel like it was set up properly for everyone to feel comfortable."

No one said anything, until finally the woman from Los Angeles said, "Just let them go. They're bringing bad energy into the space."

The impact of the shrooms was slowly wearing off. We'd managed to make it to the Whole Foods parking lot in the middle of a nice neighborhood with large homes after leaving the "ceremony," and we were sitting in the car, waiting for our trip to end.

As we regained our bearings, we both burst out laughing simultaneously.

"We just stormed out of a ceremony," David said. "A fake ceremony."

"Yes, and quite dramatically."

"That was hilarious when you think about it. You were channeling Mother Earth or something."

"And you were going through something, too," I said.

"Yeah, something related to my programming around being a victim," he responded.

"Did you even want to go to the ceremony?" I asked.

"No," he responded, "I just wanted connection."

"And this is how we got here. It's like a missed connection. We had each other but we had to go to this ceremony to see that. There's no way I could've done that ceremony alone."

"Me neither," he said.

We looked at each other and burst out laughing again.

"We're sitting in the middle of Albuquerque in the middle of the night, extremely high," I observed.

"I know," David howled. "It's hilarious. This is like Harold and Kumar—but we're in our forties."

I couldn't stop laughing. "This is the best experience we've ever had together."

David nodded. "I don't think that we've ever been closer, Christina."

"Hey, you know what this is?" I said. "This is Grandmother

energy. This is actually the Grandmother's medicine from the aya-huasca ceremony. Remember how I mentioned that my intention was to not have life that was separated from my spirituality? This is what she's showing us."

"Whoa, Christina." David's eyes widened. "Grandmother has been with us the whole time. This whole trip to Santa Fe. She's been a part of everything."

"Doesn't it feel like Grandmother? She wants her children to have fun. To enjoy life. It's not a mother's energy. Grandmother's energy is different. It's playful. This is the joy and beauty of life."

"Yes, it reminds me of the jokester energy." David shook his head. "We've been taking ourselves too seriously. We've spent so many years processing pain and trauma in our lives. Grandmother also wants us to have fun."

"And she wants us to see the connection we have around us," I added. "Like our friendship. We were there for each other the whole time. I was spending time chatting with random men I met online for support and companionship when we had each other."

"We needed this experience to see that," David said. "We needed the entire experience."

"Remember at the beginning of our trip when we said that one day this trip would make sense to us. Well, I think it makes sense now. It was about our friendship. It was to bring us closer together."

"I don't think we've ever been closer," he repeated, and I was thrilled.

"Me neither," I said.

"Just one more thing," he said. "I wish that I could push a but-ton and you could channel Mother Earth the way you did in that room. That was amazing."

"It's just about love and connection," I said, remembering the feeling I'd had before. "The land and the earth can show us every-thing we need to know."

✖ ꓲꓛ ✖

Chapter 26

Life Is a Ceremony

My prayer to the land had been answered: when fall came, I was still in Santa Fe. Not only had my casita lease been extended indefinitely, my landlord had also asked if I wanted to be the property manager for the main house in exchange for reduced rent. I had gladly accepted, recognizing that being a caretaker for homes was something I was good at–a natural part of my identity.

The casita had slowly become more and more like home. It was already furnished beautifully, so I was intentional about not creating more clutter, although I did add small touches to make it feel more like my home. I also found a job managing an art gallery, which ended up being a perfect fit for me. It paid the bills, I loved the environment, and it didn't distract me from my writing.

Between the springtime and fall, I went on a few dates, but mostly I spent time in solitude. It was different from when I'd lived in Ojai and Santa Barbara, when I was always dating and seeking a relationship. Here in Santa Fe, I was happily alone.

As things settled, I knew it was time to return to California to retrieve some of my belongings. Earlier in the year, I'd sold some of my furniture and decor to allow Chloe and her new roommates to have more control over how the apartment in Noe Valley looked. The lease was now in Chloe's name, and with that shift, the responsibilities of managing the place were no longer on my shoulders.

It was a relief to let my San Francisco apartment go. I'd recognized that holding on to one space had prevented me from building another home elsewhere, and now that I was comfortably settling into my Santa Fe space, I didn't need a back-up apartment in Noe Valley. It was time to move on—for my sake, but also for the apartment's sake.

I was still learning to connect with the energy of the land. I knew my understanding of this relationship was deepening, and that the lessons wouldn't unfold automatically. My focus was on my creativity and on nurturing my relationship to the grounded energy of the land. Friends in the Bay Area often asked to catch up by phone or Zoom, but I declined those offers. Somehow, my Santa Fe life felt too precious to let everyone in just yet. I deactivated my Facebook account, which meant I was no longer managing my women's group, and it was incredibly liberating. I began to see that all that energy I invested in inspiring and supporting others online could be rechanneled into my own creative work and into integrating my own healing. I felt free.

By the time I returned to San Francisco in September, I was ready to face my former home.

The night before I left, I had a dream about my mother. When I woke up early in the morning to head to the Albuquerque Sunport airport, the dream—and my mother's face—was still vivid in my mind.

She was beaming, even happier than I'd ever remembered her being in real life. She was sitting with me at the airport. There was some confusion at the gate. I would find myself walking toward the gate, then discover it was the wrong one and return to my mother in the food court.

I asked her if she would come back to the airport to pick me up. She smiled a huge smile and said, "I'm not sure."

I hadn't remembered her smile until I saw it in the dream; only then did I recall how powerful it must have been, and how beautiful she had been when she was happy.

"But why aren't you sure?" I asked. "You can just take my car when you leave and return when I'm back."

"I don't know if I can," she said.

I was disappointed by her uncertainty, although I wasn't sad. I didn't feel abandoned. I knew deep within my bones that if she could have said yes, she would have, and for whatever reason she wasn't able to. I thought that this was perhaps a metaphor for her death, and her presence in my life from the spiritual realm.

When I landed at San Francisco International Airport, I took in the bustling energy of the people. Everyone seemed to be moving more quickly than I was used to, and they were all walking with their heads down, staring at their phones. I could see how lost people could be in their virtual worlds. In some ways, I felt energized by the pace, but I also knew that I could never live that way again. My world in Santa Fe felt contained and small in a good way. I could walk to work in less than ten minutes, and most of the places I went to in Santa Fe were a ten-minute drive away.

Some dear friends, like Terra, had offered me a place to stay while I was in town, but I'd told Chloe I wanted to stay one final night in the apartment, and she had obliged. When I reached my old apartment, I dropped my suitcase at the bottom of the stairs, and reluctance rose up inside me; I wasn't ready to go inside. I texted Chloe and told her I'd arrived, but I would first head to Philz, up the street, for a coffee.

When I'd returned to San Francisco in the middle of the previous year, after my sojourn in Ojai and Santa Barbara, a neighborhood friend of mine had said that I couldn't have come back to San Francisco to live as the same person—that to her it seemed I had gone through a spiritual awakening. In retrospect, I could see the truth in that statement, only whatever transformation had taken place at that time was only just the beginning. Santa Fe was a continuation of what I'd begun on my journey in Southern California. The awakening was not just a moment but rather an internal and spiritual shift, and then a grounding in the physical world.

As I walked through the neighborhood, everything felt familiar but also different. Some stores had closed; others had moved to a another block; and new places had opened up, including a rotisserie right on my old block. A jewelry store was closing down. A store dedicated to making your own home scents had opened up. The flower shop down the street had taken over the neighboring storefront where there had formerly been a shoe store. My friend who had a women's fashion brand had opened up a pop-up for men's clothing. There was bustle and change. It occurred to me that neighborhoods, cities, and even homes—very much like people—weather storms, navigate ups and downs, and ultimately reinvent themselves, and all of it is an act of survival.

I still had the key to my old apartment. When I walked up the stairs, I called out Chloe's name. I didn't hear her response, so I let myself in. I peered into each of the rooms, starting with the front living room. I noticed that a black-and-white photo of my mother that I'd put on the altar during the Đám Giỗ was still on the fireplace. One of the rooms was set up like a guest room, and I assumed that Chloe had prepared it for me.

Chloe's friend, Jonathan, had moved into the room I had slept in for most of the years I had lived in the apartment. It looked so lived-in compared to when I had occupied the space. Thick cream curtains hung from the window. There were a dozen or so plants, and while there were many of them, they were tidy and organized. The back living room was also full of plants. My circular tulip table was now in the center of the room, and the futon couch I had purchased for the guest room was now their main couch. A mixture of throw blankets, some of which I recognized as mine, were folded up at the bottom of the couch. A rocking chair was in the corner, as was a generic standing lamp. A colorful abstract painting hung above the fireplace. The kitchen was a mess, with everyone's stuff everywhere.

I preferred things to be hidden, but it was no longer my home.

I walked through the laundry room and found Chloe sitting on the back porch. I felt a twinge of guilt over how I'd behaved as a roommate. She was the one who'd held down the fort, who'd navigated the emotional ups and downs that I had felt about this place over the last two years. All the tense moments flashed before my eyes, but what remained was admiration for her steady patience.

"How do you feel about all the transitions here?" I asked her.

She shrugged. "I've just sort of accepted that people are coming and going. I thought the last person would stay longer, but he was only here for a month before he moved in with friends. Carrie, who is moving in, just needs an extra place to crash in case she wants to spend some time in the city but she also has a shared place in San Jose near her work. So I don't know how often she'll stay here."

"Wild to think about how many people have been through this house over the years," I said.

"We were talking about that the other day," she said. "Must be at least a thousand—or hundreds, at least."

We went inside and lounged on the sofa in the living room. I suggested that we FaceTime our mutual friend, Sana, in the Netherlands. She'd had a baby about six weeks prior, and I still hadn't had a chance to speak with her. Without Sana, I wouldn't have ever known Chloe, and I felt a deep gratitude to both of them. They were six or seven years younger than me, still in their childbearing years. Sana had taken on motherhood as she tackled everything in her life—with the utmost attention and care. Chloe also aspired to be a mother. She'd frozen her eggs a few months earlier, and had always been open to exploring nontraditional ways of building a family, like raising a child with a good friend or in a community.

On the phone with Sana, I noticed that I was finally okay with not having children. I was happy being a witness to my friends' families. The lives they were living were not my life. I was happy for Sana, and grateful that what she was going through wasn't my path. Without entirely realizing that it was happening, I'd entered a different phase, and closing the door on what had come before felt freeing. I was focused on my creativity, my own Mother Earth energy, and all the ways that manifested in my life—before, presently, and in the future.

I booked a Zoom session with my former therapist while I was in town. Once I'd decided my stay in New Mexico would be permanent, he'd told me he wouldn't be able to work with me anymore, but he had kindly extended an offer to do periodic check-ins when I was in California.

He was familiar to me, like an old friend. He wore a wool cardigan sweater that evoked images of how he must have been as a child—curious and proper. I could also picture him with his own children, although I didn't know how many he had, and how tender he probably was with them. I felt he extended that same tenderness, care, and concern to me as his patient.

About a week before our session, I emailed him a rough update of everything that had transpired since I'd been in Santa Fe. In bullet points, I shared the details of my new life. I told him about my job at the gallery. I shared that my writing was progressing, and while I still lived a rather solitary existence, I appreciated my alone time. I was actively trying to expand my social circle and network. I was still cautious of being consumed by other people's problems and lives, so I proceeded tentatively. I acknowledged that I was still working on my ability to relate to people and maintain intimate relationships. I'd recently observed my pattern of ending relationships with people I was dating prematurely—something I'd done countless times.

When we got on Zoom, he started in. "I reread your email this morning," he said. "So I'm all caught up on everything that's going on in your life. Where would you like to start?"

I wasn't sure, actually.

"I'm happy," I said after a pause, "but I also realize how many things I've missed in my life. I can see now all the ways that people have shown me love, care, and support. And I often operated by pushing it aside. I want to do things differently. I think I can."

"For most of your life, you've been concerned about surviving," he reminded me. "Taking care of yourself by yourself and building walls to protect yourself. You're not there anymore, but that's what you had to do in the past. You had to make sure your environment and the people around you felt safe."

"Yes." I nodded. "I know that I can make these adjustments moving forward but at the same time, I kinda feel ashamed of all the endings of those relationships."

"I used to be disappointed with the pinnacles of traditional therapy," he shared. "One is simply the ability to hold complex emotions. I thought, *how boring*, but really it's quite beautiful. And challenging in many ways. We create stories and ideas to protect ourselves. But once we start realizing what we're doing, we can see the shades of gray. We can see the nuances. I think you've reached that point."

I looked at my former therapist on the screen, then glanced outside at the cloudy skies. I had reached a pinnacle, and although it was tinged with regret, I felt the complexity of my past and also compassion for my previous selves. I could see how I'd run away, how I'd left relationships—friendships even. The moment I felt afraid, the moment when I thought I might get hurt—that was often when I'd left.

The journey to arrive at this moment and realization had been a long one, but I felt I could now hold the complexity of emotions, and I didn't think I would run away as frequently—or at the very least not as fast—as I had before.

There was still a distance between my father, my sister, and me, but there was also a deeper level of understanding. I believed we were a family for a reason, and while we had all coped with the loss of my mother and lived our lives very differently, we were bound together by our wounds and our shared experiences.

I felt resolved with my father, and those healing lessons brought so many benefits to the way I began to show up in my relationships. There was still a gap for me between awareness and action, but I was on the right path.

I saw my father differently. Not only had he changed, but I had as well. I thought of the vacation he had taken us on after my mother passed away. I also thought about the times—there were only a handful—when he'd asked for my help, and I'd been too busy. I hoped our relationship would change.

Over the period of time when I was in Santa Fe, I exchanged a few texts with my sister. She'd message about her kids or would respond to one of my dad's emails to both of us. It still saddened me that we weren't close, but I didn't have any grand expectations anymore that our relationship would change—nor did I have any resentment around that reality.

What felt most significant was that I was well aware of my own flaws in relation to my family. I lived my life freely and independently. Sometimes this felt liberating and sometimes lonely. But I had accepted myself and my own path

I still hoped, but didn't expect, that one day my sister would embark on a deeper spiritual path and that we would connect more deeply then. As for my father, I was grateful for my newfound understanding and ability to feel his love—even if it had to go through my stomach to my heart.

On my healing journey, I'd learned to understand my family and my responses to them. In doing so, I'd made peace with myself—and, by extension, with them.

In San Francisco, Chloe and her roommate left for the weekend, so I had one day alone in my old apartment. It seemed meant to be—a way for me to get closure with the place.

I spent most of the time organizing boxes I had stored in the closet and going through clothes, deciding which pieces I wanted to bring with me and which ones I wanted to donate. The years I'd lived in the apartment flashed before my eyes—nearly a decade of accumulated memories and belongings. I perused journals I'd filled over the years. I came across a manuscript I'd worked on in my early thirties, the one that was mostly about my family and Vietnam. I didn't want to read some of my former words. I immediately saw through the patterns that had held me back at the time. I also noticed the obstacles that still remained with me. But at least now I could hold those memories with me as I moved forward. They didn't need to be stuffed in an old storage box.

That evening, after spending the day organizing, I slept in the living room. I loved sleeping back there because it was the quietest room in the house, and because ever since my mother's twenty-fifth-anniversary Đám Giỗ, I'd been able to feel her presence there. I could tell that she was still present in the space, and I wanted to absorb that energy while it lasted.

The next morning, when I went outside, a woman was playing the didgeridoo—an unusual instrument for someone to be playing on the street, and the same instrument the sound healer had played at my mother's Đám Giỗ–right in front of the apartment.

I remembered the first ceremony we'd hosted and how my friend's mother had told me that when the incense was fully burned, the ceremony would close. It dawned on me that maybe I'd never closed the second ceremony. Maybe I'd invited my mother back to the physical realm last year, and maybe she'd never left.

As I listened to the didgeridoo, it became clear to me that my mother had been journeying with me since that ceremony–and like that, I understood the dream I'd had before coming to San Francisco.

She'd said she didn't know if she could come back for me. What she'd meant was that she didn't know if she could continue to journey with me in this way. I hadn't felt abandoned by her in the dream because there was a deeper understanding that no matter what, she would be there with me. She may not be sure if she'd be able to join me again in the same way, but she would always be there. She lived on through me, and would always be alongside me.

She was happy. I was happy.

The ceremony was finally closing now, in San Francisco, with the playing of the didgeridoo.

I left San Francisco with two suitcases. I'd told myself as a teenager, after my mother passed away, that I wanted to travel lightly, to carry with me only two suitcases. I understood now that this declaration came from my fear–a younger version of me convincing herself that she didn't need to be attached to people or places. I believed then that it was easier to move through the world if you were free of attachments; I thought I didn't need relationships with other people to live a satisfying and meaningful existence.

The two suitcases, well, that wasn't such bad advice. But in hindsight, I would revise my younger self's message to this: It's great to be a minimalist and not have too many belongings. But

The Veil Between Two Worlds

people, we need them. And even if they might leave us prematurely, like my mother did, they can still journey with us. And while there are many ways—through ceremonies, for example—that we might intentionally connect with other realms, there's also a lot of beauty in the physical world. There are also so many people in this realm, right here, who are ready to walk alongside us.

Life, after all, is one big ceremony.

Epilogue

A fresh snow blanketed the ground. Of all the seasons I had experienced in Santa Fe, I realized I loved the winter the most. I had come to appreciate my Vietnamese middle name, Tuyết, which means snow, even more. Snow felt like peace to me, a blanket of white wonderment gently settled on the ground. It represented the peacefulness that I had been seeking—that I had finally found within myself.

Home, I recognized, is a physical place in the world, but it's also a place we find within ourselves—warm, comforting, and nurturing. I had also come to the realization that whatever I created on the inside with my mind and heart was reflected externally in the world. My prayer to the land had been answered: I'd gotten to experience all the seasons in Santa Fe.

And, more importantly, I'd been allowed to continue to learn to work with the energy of the land, to deepen my connection to Mother Earth.

By the time I saw David again in Santa Fe, exactly one year had passed since we'd first ventured there. Two of our mutual friends were visiting from DC, and they'd rented the house next to my casita for a week. David and I hadn't been in touch much since he'd left Santa Fe, although when big realizations hit me, I of course reached out to share them with him.

In the last year, he'd returned to the Bay Area for a few months, then spent five or six months in Mexico, where he was planning to move permanently.

When David and I had a moment alone to catch up, there was so much I wanted to say, but at the same time I simply appreciated his energy—it was enough just to be with him. He told me how his spiritual life was developing in Mexico. He also shared that he'd seen Diego, the shaman from the Albuquerque ceremony, but hadn't said anything to him. I told him there must be some meaning there—something to uncover or learn.

He also spoke about how he wasn't confident recommending Saanvi's community to anyone because a few of his friends had experienced challenges with her. A part of me sighed a big sigh of relief: he was taking his spiritual life into his own hands, recognizing and coming to the realization of his own unique gifts and talents. I felt the old feeling of us being on parallel motorbikes. He didn't know if he would ever return to live permanently in the States. His plan was to spend some time in Mexico, and then maybe Vietnam.

"Who knows," he joked, "maybe you'll be back in Vietnam by then too."

The chatty little sister came through me immediately, and I excitedly opined about how life had unfolded so magically for me in Santa Fe.

His response, while simple, landed straight in my heart: "I love your journey here, Christina."

David had always been my sacred mirror. We were stepping into our spiritual authority and finding ways to express and claim that authority in the world. I saw now how even my judgment of him while we'd traveled together had actually been judgment of myself. There had been another layer of my own spiritual growth that I had yet to claim, and David had helped me see that. I was grateful to have him as a friend, a spiritual sibling, and a witness to so many important moments of my journey.

I couldn't imagine navigating either of the two worlds I lived in—the physical or the spiritual—without him.

Acknowledgments

Some scenes from this memoir were written years ago. Over time, our memories unfold and change when we revisit them. I have told this story to the best of my ability as I have processed and healed certain scenes from my past. I've changed names and some descriptions of people, places, and experiences to protect identities and, in some cases, sacred work. I honor those who have come across my path, and those experiences that I've shared here—some of them painful—that have ultimately turned into growth and healing. I am so grateful for each and every one of my experiences, and for the people I've been blessed to know.

I'm so thankful, too, for my family—my mother, my father, and my sister—for we are a nuclear unit for a reason. Our souls chose one another, and I'm honored to be on this journey with all of you.

To my dear friend whom this book highlights: You will always be one of my most treasured friends. You have helped me uncover so much about myself. I honestly don't know if I would understand myself at this level if it weren't for our friendship. Thank you as well to countless other dear friends who helped along the way simply by being there, reading my lengthy emails, and helping me to process my experiences.

The Veil Between Two Worlds

Finally, I'm deeply indebted to Brooke Warner for her support and guidance throughout this process. Her memoir writing class helped me to find consistency and rhythm in my writing routine, and her subsequent editorial guidance enabled me to weave my tapestry of memories into a cohesive narrative.

About the Author

Christina Vo is a writer who previously worked for international organizations in Vietnam and Switzerland and also ran a floral design business in San Francisco. *The Veil Between Two Worlds* is her first book. Vo currently resides in Santa Fe, New Mexico.

SELECTED TITLES FROM SHE WRITES PRESS

She Writes Press is an independent publishing company
founded to serve women writers everywhere.
Visit us at www.shewritespress.com.

Bless the Birds: Living with Love in a Time of Dying by Susan J. Tweit. $16.95, 978-1-64742-036-9. Writer Susan Tweit and her economist-turned-sculptor husband Richard Cabe had just settled into their version of a "good life" when Richard saw thousands of birds one day—harbingers of the brain cancer that would kill him two years later. This intimate memoir chronicles their journey into the end of his life, framed by their final trip together: a 4,000-mile, long-delayed honeymoon road trip.

This Trip Will Change Your Life: A Shaman's Story of Spirit Evolution by Jennifer B. Monahan. $16.95, 978-1-63152-111-9. One woman's inspirational story of finding her life purpose and the messages and training she received from the spirit world as she became a shamanic healer.

Nothing But Blue: A Memoir by Diane Lowman. $16.95, 978-1-63152-402-8. In the summer of 1979, Diane Meyer Lowman, a nineteen-year-old Middlebury College student, embarked on a ten-week working trip aboard a German container ship with a mostly male crew. The voyage would forever change her perspective on the world—and her place in it.

Mani/Pedi: A True-Life Rags-to-Riches Story by Krista Beth Driver. $16.95, 978-1-63152-626-8. After Saigon fell, Charlie was faced with a critical decision: stay in Vietnam under communist rule, or risk everything to escape with her children and set out for a better future in America. Against all odds, she managed to get herself, her husband, and her two small children out of Vietnam—and went on to build a life more incredible than she ever imagined possible.

When the Red Gates Opened: A Memoir of China in the 1980s by Dori Jones Yang. $16.95, 978-1-63152-751-7. In the 1980s, after decades of isolation, China opened its doors—and Communism changed forever. As a foreign correspondent during this pivotal era, Dori Jones fell in love with China and with a Chinese ma; this memoir recalls the euphoria of Americans discovering a new China, as well as the despair of Tiananmen.

How Sweet the Bitter Soup: A Memoir by Lori Qian. $16.95, 978-1-63152-614-5. After accepting an exciting job offer—teaching at a prestigious school in China—Lori found herself in Guangzhou, China, where she fell in love with the culture and with a man from a tiny town in Hubei province. What followed was a transformative adventure—one that will inspire readers to use the bitter to make life even sweeter.

CPSIA information can be obtained
at www.ICGtesting.com
Printed in the USA
JSHW020730240523
42173JS00001B/1